Mikael Berndtsson • Jörgen Hansson
Björn Olsson • Björn Lundell

Thesis Projects

A Guide for Students in Computer Science and Information Systems

Second Edition

 Springer

Mikael Berndtsson
University of Skövde
Sweden

Jörgen Hansson
Software Engineering Institute
Carnegie Mellon University
Pittsburgh, PA
USA

Björn Olsson
University of Skövde
Sweden

Björn Lundell
University of Skövde
Sweden

British Library Cataloguing in Publication Data
A catalogue record for this book is available from the British Library

Library of Congress Control Number: 2007936686

ISBN-13: 978-1-84800-008-7   e-ISBN-13: 978-1-84800-009-4

Printed on acid-free paper

© Springer-Verlag London Limited 2008
First edition Springer-Verlag London Limited 2002, 1-85233-332-4

9 8 7 6 5 4 3 2 1

Springer Science+Business Media
springer.com

Preface

Any B.Sc. or M.Sc. study programme in the computing discipline typically ends with a capstone project. A capstone project builds and tests the skills and the knowledge acquired during the education and is an essential part of the training towards becoming a professional. There is a large number of different terms for these types of projects: capstone project, senior project, final year project, B.Sc./ M.Sc. thesis project, etc. In this book we will use the term 'thesis project', and in some cases, for the sake of simplicity, just 'project'.

This book focuses on thesis projects within the computing discipline. Thus, the type of project discussed in this book is in line with the capstone format described in the ACM/IEEE Computing Curricula 2001 Computer Science (p. 53):

> ... an alternative capstone format is a research experience that includes some original work, a review of the scientific literature, and an investigation of a proposed solution, followed by a scientific paper and/or an oral presentation of the results. It is important to remember that these are undergraduates and be realistic about the amount and quality of research expected. Even so, it may be more worthwhile to expose outstanding students to the challenges of research than to have them design and build yet another program

In this book, we present a process for conducting thesis projects with the research-orientation described in the quote above. This process was developed at the University of Skövde, Sweden, and it has been applied successfully at the B.Sc. and M.Sc. levels and to a wide spectrum of projects, addressing many different subjects within computing. Typical subject areas have included, for example, artificial intelligence, theoretical computer science, databases, data communication, distributed systems, human-computer interaction, operating systems, real-time systems, web technologies, software engineering, systems analysis and technology transfer. Some projects have been theoretical and others more empirically oriented, and they have included both science- and technology-oriented projects. In addition to this book, the interested reader can also find additional information on our experiences of these types of projects in the following article:

> Olsson, B., Berndtsson, M., Lundell, B. and Hansson, J. (2003). Running research-oriented final year projects for CS and IS students. In *Proceedings of the 34th SIGCSE Technical Symposium on Computer Science Education*, Reno, Nevada, USA, 19–23 February 2003, pp. 79–83, ACM Press.

Who Should Read This Book?

We have written this book with the aim of meeting the needs of students who are close to finishing a B.Sc. or M.Sc. degree. However, several other categories of readers may find this book a valuable companion. We hope that a number different categories of readers may benefit from the book, as outlined below.

- Students who plan to do a B.Sc. or M.Sc. project in which they are expected to: use scientific methods to solve a problem, work with a research-oriented focus, write a report in the form of a thesis, and/or present and defend their work orally (viva voce examination).
- Supervisors who supervise B.Sc. or M.Sc. projects. It is important that supervisors are familiar with and up to date on questions and issues that students might encounter in the various phases of their B.Sc. and M.Sc. projects.
- Examiners of research-oriented B.Sc. or M.Sc. projects. The book may be particularly useful for anyone who is new in the role as examiner and needs a head start on, for example, assessment criteria.
- Coordinators who are responsible for maintaining and developing course curricula for B.Sc. or M.Sc. projects, as well as other people involved in development of study programmes.

In addition to the general descriptions and advice provided in this book, we want to emphasise that it is important for students to find out the exact requirements at the department where the project is undertaken.

Changes from Previous Edition

- *Terminology*. We have updated the terminology and do not use the term *Final Year Project*. Instead we either use the more term *Thesis Project* or simply just projects.
- *Information-seeking and use*. A new chapter on *Information-seeking and use* and a subsection called *Improve your learning (and grade)* have been added to strengthen the material on how to search for relevant literature and also how to validate it. This material was written by Ola Pilerot, who is lecturer at the Swedish School of Library and Information Science (SSLIS) at Göteborg University and at University College of Borås.
- *Nuts and bolts*. We have fine tuned the text and updated the information wherever appropriate.

Acknowledgements

This book would not have been possible without the support of a number of people, all of whom we wish to acknowledge with gratitude for their help and support. We are indebted to all our fellow examiners, supervisors and students who, during the period 1996–2007, improved the quality of the thesis project process. We would also like to thank Stig Emanuelsson, Anders Malmsjö, Pam Lings, Dan Lundh, Lars Niklasson, Ingi Jonasson, and Ola Pilerot for their support and assistance during our work on preparing this book, and Lars-Erik Johansson for his encouragement and support in the initial phase of this project.

We are grateful to the University of Skövde and the Department of Computer and Information Science, Linköping University for their financial support, and to our friends at Springer-Verlag London Ltd, who have been very patient and understanding during the development of this book. Finally, our special thanks go to our families.

June 2007
Mikael Berndtsson
Jörgen Hansson
Björn Olsson
Björn Lundell

Contents

Part II   Process

Part I
Concepts

1
Introduction

One of the strongest instincts we have is the desire to learn new things about the world we live in. In fact, through our entire life we never stop learning new things. This has been crucial for our survival, but it also stimulates our curiosity. Very young children learn by copying the behaviour of others. Learning is later extended to acquiring knowledge through other modes of communication, e.g. through books, lectures and labs. One of the primary goals of academic training is to learn how to learn, i.e. to learn how to continuously absorb new knowledge. This is increasingly important in rapidly changing areas such as computer science and information systems. The process of exploring the unknown, studying and learning new things, building new knowledge about things that no one has understood before – that is what we think of as performing research. Undertaking a thesis project is one step towards an increased understanding of how to study, how to learn about complex phenomena, and towards learning how to build new knowledge about the world around us.

A thesis project is a capstone in undergraduate and graduate education, and as such, it builds and tests the skills and knowledge acquired during your education and training to become professionals. The thesis project is different from a traditional course in several ways; in its size, in its goals, in the form of examination, in the form of supervision and in the form of communication (personal dialogue, as opposed to lectures). A project represents a significantly larger workload than a single course. While traditional courses include lectures and lab work, where the focus is on acquiring knowledge in a specific subject area, the thesis project focuses on deepening your understanding of a subject. But above all, it should give you training in carrying out projects independently, at an advanced level, using a sound method.

This introductory chapter sets the scene for the book, discusses the characteristics of thesis projects, and explains how best to use this book in order to complete your project successfully.

M. Berndtsson et al. (eds.), *Thesis Projects: A Guide for Students in Computer Science and Information Systems.*
© Springer 2008

1.1   Motivation and Purpose of the Book

According to the ACM/IEEE Computing Curricula 2005 there are five major computing disciplines: Computer engineering, Computer science, Information systems, Information technology, and Software engineering. Although the material covered in this book is applicable to all five computing disciplines, we will focus on examples related to computer science and information systems.

Computer science and information systems are two areas spanning a wide range of topics, for example, artificial intelligence, CASE-tools, database systems, human-computer interaction, information systems assessment, programming languages, operating systems, and web based information systems. The areas are multi-disciplinary in the sense that they have elements from the natural sciences (mathematics, logic etc.) and human sciences (psychology, philosophy etc.). The multi-disciplinary nature of the covered areas does not simplify the task of performing a project; indeed it presents profound challenges and interesting problems. Areas such as social science, psychology, mathematics, and engineering have established guidelines and methods for formulating problems, and for choosing appropriate research methods.

The wide range of areas within computer science and information systems means that it is not always easy to formulate a problem that is suitable for a project, to choose the appropriate research method, or to develop a structure for a written report. Furthermore, many students experience uncertainty as to what to expect from a project, how to complete it within the given time frame, and how to attain the goals of the project. This is understandable since most students will have had no prior experience of a project as complex and as broad in scope as a thesis project. It is difficult to envisage what it will be like. These concerns are due partly to the lack of suitable textbooks and the lack of references specifically targeting students doing projects in computer science and information systems. Moreover, the project is probably the biggest project you, as a student, will have undertaken in your academic life, and maybe even in your life.

This book focuses on the process of carrying out a project, with a particular emphasis on the roles and responsibilities of the student, the supervisor and the examiner. The aim of the book is to bridge the gap between different research methods and describe the general process of carrying out a project in the computing disciplines. In this book we identify a series of actions that should be of assistance to you when planning and carrying out your project.

1.2   Purposes of Thesis Projects

What characterises a project is the fact that it is something that is planned, has a specific purpose, lasts only for a limited time with a clear start and finish, and is undertaken with finite resources with respect to personnel, money and equipment.

You can view the thesis project as serving several (sometimes overlapping) purposes:

- *Learning more.* The project is an opportunity for studying a subject in more depth.
- A *stepping stone towards finding and securing a job.* You may view the project as preparation for working life, by practising your skills and knowledge on real-world problems.
- A *stepping stone towards graduate studies.* You may use the project as preparation for graduate studies, by exploring a research problem and learning about the research process.

In addition, your university probably sees your project as serving two further purposes. Typically, these can be captured by the following goals, shared by most projects, and which emphasise the educational motivation and the research motivation.

The first goal is the "educational" part of the project. This can be viewed as a test to show that you have mastered previously attained knowledge and skills, and know how they can be applied to a problem that is more realistic than those normally presented in courses. In detail, the "educational" part has the following set of learning goals. The project should (1) develop your critical thinking; (2) enhance your ability to work independently; (3) increase your understanding of how to use and appreciate scientific methods as tools for problem solving; and (4) develop your presentation skills, oral as well as written. With "critical thinking" we mean the ability to approach something new in a systematic and logical way, and to use creative and diverse, yet systematic ways to approach and solve a problem. Further, to support opinions with trustworthy evidence, data and logical reasoning; and also the ability to decide how a problem fits into a larger context. Those who have become comfortable with thinking in this way can often apply these acquired skills also in everyday life.

The second goal is the "research" part of the project, in which you will deepen your understanding of the subject area, and contribute to the common knowledge and understanding of the subject area. However, to attain this goal, your project must have aspects that are original. In other words, it is generally not enough to repeat the work of others, since it is regarded as a waste of resources (time, money etc), unless, that is, your purpose is to confirm or reject previous findings. The gains from your project are based on the contribution it makes, i.e. the development of knowledge and results that were not known before you started the project, and on the fact that the findings will have been disseminated. Dissemination of results is necessary in order to ensure that the knowledge is spread to other people working in the field. Even though you might learn a lot from the project, no one else will do so if the results are not disseminated. In this case, the project would fail to fulfil the first goal concerning the development of knowledge, i.e. to increase our understanding of the subject area. The non-dissemination of new and valuable knowledge may be said to be as useful as work not done at all.

In universities, most research is carried out by faculty members and doctoral students. However, there are many valuable reasons for linking research and undergraduate teaching. It introduces students to the fascinating world of science, and makes the latest knowledge available to them. In fact, you should expect that university studies, wherever appropriate and possible, incorporates the findings of the latest research. It is generally considered that incorporating elements of research methodology, and giving students the opportunity to undertake their own research related project, or to be involved in a bigger research project, facilitates individual students' development towards becoming independent and critically thinking people. It is our opinion that thesis projects offer excellent opportunities for closing the gap between research and teaching.

Of course, the link benefits you as a student in many ways. Not only are teachers able to pass on their knowledge and experience in the topic area, as well as research methods, but it also gives an excellent opportunity for you to become involved in leading-edge research activities. Independently of whether you do your project off-campus or in the university environment, you will notice that you will be working more closely with faculty members, and very often in a more collegial and informal way than is normally the case in traditional courses. As mentioned before, the project itself gives insights into what research is and how it is performed, and is a good preparation for doctoral studies, since it includes initial training in using research methods.

1.3   Actors in the Project

The three main actors in the project are you (the student), the supervisor and the examiner. Of the three actors, you are the most important, since you are the one who moves the project forward. You focus on solving some well-defined problem in a specific area, and thereby increase your understanding of the area. But you also learn methods that can be used to approach, structure and solve complex problems.

The supervisor is your ally. He or she should not only give you advice to help you achieve success in your project, but will also critically point out strengths and weaknesses. Normally he or she is a domain expert in the area in which you are doing your project. The dialogue between you and the supervisor serves as a compass for establishing directions when exploring new areas.

In contrast, the examiner is the person who critically evaluates your work, and recommends or decides the grade. The examiner is not necessarily a domain expert in the specific topic of your work, but normally has a good understanding of the subject area generally. More importantly, the examiner has significant experience, enabling him or her to review your work with respect to both content and method.

A positive interaction between these three actors is vital for the successful completion of a project. Note that while these are three distinct roles and are usually performed by three different people, the roles of supervisor and examiner may sometimes be carried out by the same person. However, there are many advantages of keeping the roles strictly separate.

1.4   Process

You now know what the different purposes of a project are, and who the actors involved are. The final thing you need to know before you embark on your project, is how to structure your work in order to reach the goals. The view put forward in this book is that you need to apply a process that can guide you through the various stages of the project, and at the same time help you to achieve its purposes. Therefore, the later parts of his book will outline such a process. The process involves the following steps:

1. Developing your project proposal (Chap. 5)
2. Developing your problem description (Chaps. 7 and 8)
3. Following the objectives (Chap. 9)
4. Presenting and analysing your data (Chap. 10)
5. Drawing your conclusions and identifying future work (Chap. 11)
6. Presenting and defending your work orally (Chap. 12)
7. Preparing the final version of your report (Chap. 12)

In order to ensure that your work is on track, your examiner and supervisor evaluate your work during the process. The number of checkpoints varies from university to university. If present, such checkpoints typically come after steps (1), (2) and (5). The first two checkpoints assess the quality of the project proposal and the problem description. The third checkpoint is the last quality control before the work is presented and defended. The reason for these early checkpoints is based on experience; a good start is facilitated by a strong project proposal and problem description. If the project has a good problem description with clear goals, then the rest of the work becomes easier,since it makes it easier to keep focused. Finally, after step (7) there is a final examination where the examiner recommends or decides the grade for your work.

1.5   Assessment Criteria

When doing a project, it is important to familiarise yourself with the criteria and expected standards defined by your university and/or department. In the process outlined in this book, the assessment of projects involves a set of criteria (see below) that has been shown to be representative of many departments.

General

- Relevance of chosen topic
- Originality of chosen topic
- Significance of findings
- Degree to which the work is the student's own work (as opposed to the supervisor)

Report

- Clarity of presentation
- Consistency between different parts of the report
- Degree of insight apparent from the arguments presented to support the decisions made in the project
- Ability to differentiate between others' thoughts and your own
- Ability to handle references and citations
- General stylistic impression

Defence

- Degree of insight apparent from the arguments presented to support claims and conclusions
- Degree of insight apparent from discussion in response to relevant questions

Other

- How the student performed as opponent
- Fulfilment of deadlines and other formal requirements

These criteria are discussed in more detail in later chapters, especially in Chap. 15.

1.6   Reading Guidelines

The book is divided into three parts, structured as follows. The first part of the book (Chaps. 1–3) gives a general introduction to projects. It discusses their purpose, in particular highlighting the characteristics of projects performed in academia and industry. In addition, it gives an introduction to what science is, and elaborates on the roles of the student, supervisor and the examiner. Each chapter in this section is independent, and they can be read in any order, although preferably they should all be read before the second part of the book.

The second part (Chaps. 4–12) describes in detail the process of carrying out a project. The chapters should be read sequentially since they are chronologically ordered with respect to the main stages of the project.

The third part (Chaps. 13–15) contains a set of supplementary chapters that present advice on how to search for relevant information, how to write a report, and guidelines for examiners and supervisors on how to examine projects.

The book is best read sitting in a quiet room with a nice cup of tea!

2

Computer Science and Information Systems Research Projects

This book outlines a general process for carrying out thesis projects, and it embraces the following components as fundamentally important: (1) identifying the question/research problem; (2) planning time and resources; and (3) choosing a research method for studying the specific question. In this section, we consider how a thesis project relates to research and research methods. First, we discuss the different areas within computer science and information systems.

2.1 The Landscape of CS and IS

Computer science and information systems have been described and defined in many different ways in the literature. One illuminating characterisation of computer science, given by Edsger W. Dijkstra, is as follows: "Computer science is no more about computers than astronomy is about telescopes." However, to avoid being too abstract for our purposes with this text, we will avoid in-depth elaboration of the various characterisations and definitions. Instead, we give one general view, which we then illustrate with specific examples of problems. These serve to give some idea of the broad scope of computer science and information systems.

The 1975 ACM Turing Award winners Allen Newell and Herbert A. Simon (Newell and Simon, 1976) characterised computer science (CS) as an empirical discipline, in which each new artefact, e.g. a program, can be seen as an experiment, the structure and behaviour of which can be studied. In particular, the field of computer science is concerned with a number of different issues seen from a technological perspective, e.g. theoretical aspects, such as numerical analysis, data structures and algorithms; how to store and manipulate data (e.g. by means of a database system); the relationship between different pieces of software (i.e. different types of architecture, such as client-server, peer-to-peer, two-tier, three-tier); techniques and tools for developing software (i.e. software engineering, programming languages and operating systems).

The field of Information Systems (IS), as characterised by Allen S. Lee (2001), is concerned with the interaction between social and technological issues. In other

M. Berndtsson et al. (eds.), *Thesis Projects: A Guide for Students in Computer Science and Information Systems.*
© Springer 2008

words, it is a field which focuses on the actual "link" between the human and social aspects (within an organisation or other broader social setting), *and* the hardware, software and data aspects of information technology (IT). Similarly, the IFIP Working Group 8.2, which focuses on information systems, describes its scope as being concerned with:

> the generation and dissemination of descriptive and normative knowledge about the development and use of information technologies in organisational contexts, both broadly defined. By information technology (IT), we mean technologies that can be used to store, transfer, process or represent information. By organisational context, we mean the institutional arrangements in which information is used or created (IFIP WG 8.2, 1996)

The following three examples of research problems, all of which are centred around a specific IT product such as a CASE-tool, illustrate that the primary concern for each problem might be different. Research problems that focus on the human and organisational aspects of CASE-tools are naturally IS-oriented, whereas research problems that focus on technical aspects of CASE-tools are more CS-oriented. It follows, therefore, that there will be different choices of methods available for each.

The first problem is based on a human and organisational perspective on specific types of software tools (CASE tools). The second problem is illustrated by a focus on both technical and human issues in the context of CASE tools. The third problem has a technological basis, and addresses technical aspects of CASE:

1. What are the critical elements that shape the organisational changes associated with the adoption and use of CASE tools? (Orlikowski, 1993, p. 310)
2. What features do software developers want from OO-CASE tools? Related to that question is: how well do current OO-CASE tools meet these needs? (Post and Kagan, 2000, p. 384)
3. In this paper the meta-CASE system KOGGE will be described. In order to illustrate the KOGGE approach it will be shown how KOGGE was used to implement a CASE tool supporting the object-oriented method BON. (Ebert et al., 1997, p. 203)

2.2   What is Research?

The term "research" is semantically overloaded given its use in everyday language. In an academic context, research is used to refer to the activity of a diligent and systematic inquiry or investigation in an area, with the objective of discovering or revising facts, theories, applications etc. The goal is to discover and disseminate new knowledge. While you, as a student, are learning new things throughout the course of a project, it is the goal is also that your results should include som elements of new scientific knowledge.

Science primarily aims to develop knowledge previously unknown in the area of concern, i.e. the outcome of the scientific research process should be an original contribution of knowledge to mankind. Therefore, the overall goal of scientific research is to reduce, or even eliminate uncertainty in what we know. Such results are primarily disseminated via scientific journals and conferences (c.f. the journalist who is normally said to be carrying out research when collecting material for an article. This is not considered research in a scientific sense).

To contrast scientific research with research and development (R&D) activities, which are undertaken within commercial organisations, it is instructive to look at the goals. You will see that they are different in terms of motivations and activities. In a scientific research project, the primary objective is to learn and understand complex phenomena. For example, a research institute will undertake research activities which:

- Establish new knowledge which is made available to the public, often by means of publications in academic journals or conferences
- Are not driven by profit; researchers are therefore relatively free to identify and define their research questions

In a commercial setting, there is usually an expectation that the research activities will be centred on business goals, with the aim of contributing to new products or services, which are expected to generate profit for the organisation. For example, an R&D division within an organisation might perform activities such as:

- Undertaking research in areas related to the long term business goals
- Monitoring and observing research findings and trends in technology
- Undertaking pilot-projects to analyse and evaluate new technologies
- Exploring trends in technology for their potential adoption by the organisation (e.g. to analyse whether a specific research finding, such as a new software architecture, would be suitable for adoption)
- Building research prototypes and platforms for evaluating technologies, and possibly provide the foundation infrastructure for forthcoming development efforts
- Acting as experts and technology champions within the same organisation

For example, if an IS development organisation initiates a systems development activity, a primary goal will be the resulting successful system. In contrast, if a research institution has a goal of investigating a research question, which involves developing a system, then the system itself becomes a means by which the issue is explored. In other words, the developed system is, in itself, not of primary interest.

Although the term research is used in a number of ways with different meanings, in this book we take it to mean a systematic problem solving activity, undertaken with care and concern in the context of the situation at hand. In the process of fulfilling the requirements, the research activity is characterised by the researcher's trustworthiness, both with regard to the actual *process* of undertaking the research, and to the actual *phenomenon* being studied.

Research questions state what you want to learn. Hypotheses, in contrast, are statements of your tentative answers to these questions. Many researchers explicitly state their ideas about tentative answers as part of the process of theorising and analysing data. These are often called propositions rather than hypotheses, but they have the same function, and therefore we use the term hypothesis throughout the text, to denote both meanings.

Research projects normally start with a basic question that you want to study. The question should be central to the project, thus helping to maintain the focus on the purpose of the project.

Research questions are normally, at an initial stage, more general and open. It is natural, as the project progresses, for the question to become more refined and particularised. Hence, the project is adapted to reflect an increased understanding of the problem.

2.3   Research Methods

Once you have a specific question suitable for study in a project, the next step is to choose an appropriate, systematic method. This is important for the successful completion of the project. In essence, the use of a systematic method is the soul of research.

Generally speaking, a method represents the means, procedure or technique used to carry out some process in a logical, orderly, and systematic way. In the context of a research project, a method refers to an organised approach to problem-solving that includes (1) collecting data, (2) formulating a hypothesis or proposition, (3) testing the hypothesis, (4) interpreting results, and (5) stating conclusions that can later be evaluated independently by others. This is also commonly described as the scientific method. In fact, part of the purpose of carrying out a thesis project is to get training in the use of a scientific method, which can then be applied when structuring and solving more complex problems. More importantly, you should know how, as well as why, the steps in the method are carried out. It should be pointed out that it is the nature of the problem or phenomenon itself, which guides the decision as to which method to use. Hence, you choose and use tools once you have established what you are dealing with (the nature of the problem), and when you know what you want to accomplish (hypothesis/proposition testing).

For a certain class of problems with similar characteristics (in terms of, e.g. the purpose, context, or research question) particular methods have shown to be effective in avoiding threats to validity. This is because researchers working on similar problems often interact with each other and form a community, where certain practices and norms evolve and become established.

However, given the many different methods that could be adopted within different areas of computer science and information systems, you should discuss the choice of method with your supervisor. Your supervisor has, after all, training and experience in research.

Most methods have some common characteristics, including the existence of a problem that needs to be formulated, aims and objectives to be met, and a phase where the problem will be investigated. This book does not discuss different scientific methods at length. However, related to method is methodology, which in certain areas, e.g. information systems, is commonly referred to as method. The term methodology actually comes from an old Greek word, denoting the practice of analysing different methods, implying a set or system of methods, principles, and rules for regulating a given discipline.

When we study a problem, as investigators as well as participants in a study, we approach it, for better or for worse, with certain a priori conceptions, values and experiences. These affect the way we perceive the research question. It is always the primary goal for any outcome of a project to be trustworthy, i.e. the results should be valid, independently of our personal experiences. Research methods help us to ensure validity. There are a number of potential threats to validity that have to be taken into account. It is important, therefore, that you are aware of the variety of the different types of threats to validity, which can occur in the actual application of the chosen research method. It is also important to be aware that there are slight variations in the way you can deal with different threats, even though it is partly dependent on the type of method being used in your specific project. Later in this book, we discuss the different kinds of threats to validity in more detail.

Quantitative methods have their origin in the natural sciences, where the scientific concern is with attaining an understanding of how something is constructed, how it is built, or how it works. In the natural sciences, the attempt to express this understanding by means of simple laws or principles of general importance. The research is generally driven by hypotheses, which are formulated and tested rigorously, with the goal of showing that the hypothesis is wrong. Hence, one attempts to falsify the hypothesis, and if the hypothesis withstands the test, it is considered to be correct until proven otherwise. Repeatability of the experiments and testing of hypotheses are vital to the reliability of the results, since they offer multiple opportunities for scrutinising the findings. The goal of quantitative research and methods is develop models, theories, and hypotheses pertaining to natural phenomena. The quantitative aspect is to emphasize that measurement is fundamental since it gives the connection between observation and the formalization of the model, theory and hypothesis.

Qualitative methods have their roots in the social sciences, and are primarily concerned with increasing our understanding of an area, rather than producing an explanation for it. Qualitative research is typically used in specific social contexts. Over the years, many different styles and variations of qualitative research methods have been proposed in the literature.

Qualitative research is often associated with fieldwork and analysis in a limited number of organisational settings. For example, a problem is often studied in a unique setting, and the researcher undertakes the analysis from a position close to the subject under study. He or she takes an insider's perspective, and is thereby part of the problem situation. As such, problems are often analysed by means of investigating and interpreting human or organisational aspects in relation to technology. In undertaking such research, the organisational context itself changes. As humans and organisational conditions change over time, the pre-condition for the study and the analysis of the problem change. Hence, repeatability of experiments may not be possible.

Even though there is much in common between different kinds of validity threats independently of the type of research, there are specific research methods and styles of research which are associated with certain strategies for addressing potential threats to validity. Later in this book, we review a few of the most likely in qualitative research.

By observing and reflecting on your own and others' experiences of research projects, you will develop an increased sensitivity to potential traps. This is important, since your success depends on how well potential threats are taken into account. It has a direct bearing on what can be claimed in your findings. In other words, addressing validity is closely related to minimising the limitations of the findings in the project. When discussing methods later in this book (Chap. 8), we shall make additional comments on validity threats, and in particular, how they can be identified and dealt with.

2.4   Linkage Between Research and Thesis Projects

Up to now, we have elaborated on research and its relationship with development activities in different environments, ranging from scientific research carried out at research institutes, via research and development, to product development in industrial and organisational settings. While the notion of research and the outcome may differ in these environments, a core aspect is the systematic process by which such activities are undertaken. It is our view that thesis projects share this core aspect, even if the outcome is not necessarily intended as a scientific contribution. It is also our view that thesis projects should have a stronger emphasis on developing your own learning. This concerns your ability to carry out a bigger project systematically and independently, to apply previously acquired knowledge, and to acquire new indepth knowledge in the project area. Our notion of research, in the context of thesis projects, simply denotes a structured process for solving complex problems, formulated as research questions.

During your project, you interact with examiners and supervisors who are trained in carrying out research. You will be inspired and influenced by the strategies they use when approaching and tackling problems. The nature of the problem, which will be the topic of your thesis, might be of a scientific nature, or it might originate in a purely industrial setting. In either case, you will benefit from using this systematic way of identifying and addressing a suitable research problem.

3
Actors Involved, their Roles and Relationships

The purpose of this chapter is to discuss the roles of the people involved in your project, emphasise their responsibilities and elaborate on their inter-relationships. The roles of the participants in your project can be characterised as follows:

- The student, who identifies, approaches and solves a problem
- The supervisor, who guides you in your work
- The examiner, who critically assesses your work

The number of people involved in your project may vary, since a project may include multiple students, or supervisors. In fact, your project may even have multiple examiners, although this is not very common for student projects at bachelor and master's level. Normally, a thesis project has one student, one supervisor and one examiner. A project with more than one person in each role introduces additional issues that need to be addressed, and these will be discussed separately.

As mentioned earlier, projects are characterised by the fact that they have a distinct start and end, and hence, a limited time in which they can be performed. Projects are allocated resources (people, time, money etc). Furthermore, projects have distinct purposes, and aim to achieve defined goals. Hence, carrying out a project is the task of optimising the use of these resources, and of delivering the results.

3.1 The Student

As you know, you are the one who moves the project forward. Without your initiative and commitment, the work will not be progressing satisfactorily, and the project comes to a halt. Supervisors have the right to expect a high level of commitment from their students, who in turn should respond positively to advice and guidance. In so doing, students develop an increasing level of independence when it comes to solving complex problems.

You should always remember that your supervisor is your best friend when doing a project. He or she believes in you. Otherwise they would not have agreed

M. Berndtsson et al. (eds.), *Thesis Projects: A Guide for Students in Computer Science and Information Systems.*

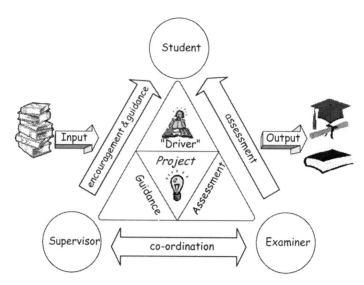

Fig. 3.1 The three actors and how they are related. Clip arts © 2000–2007 www.arttoday.com

to be your supervisor in the first place. The supervisor is there to help you, pointing out both the good aspects in your work and the less good ones, in order to help you improve. You are both involved in a project which may increase the body of knowledge and deepen our understanding of a problem in a particular area. This is the ultimate reward for a successful project, but it requires that you are both committed to doing a good job (Fig. 3.1). Your supervisor certainly is!

3.1.1 The Responsibilities of the Student

As a student you should:

- Discuss with your supervisor what kind of guidance you find most useful, and what your possible preferences might be with respect to the working routines
- Plan and discuss with your supervisor the topic of the project and the timetable, including a schedule of meetings where appropriate feedback can be given
- Maintain progress according to the agreed schedule, and continuously report your progress to the supervisor
- Keep systematic records of work completed
- Make sure to submit written material to your supervisor in time to allow for discussion and comments before proceeding to the next stage of the project
- Decide on a date, together with your supervisor, when the project should be finished and the report submitted to the department or university

- Discuss with your supervisor (taking into account any input from the supervisor) the preparation of the report, and decide when it is ready for submission
- Write up and submit the report within the time limit, and in accordance with local submission guidelines
- Address and respond to criticism, guidance, and suggestions given by the supervisor, which may include undertaking any study required by the supervisor, e.g. directed reading or applying a statistical test to analyse your data
- Be informed about and respect any regulations and considerations, legal as well as ethical, that are relevant for the project
- Drive the project forward and initiate discussions
- Inform your supervisor of any problems or difficulties, technical as well as non-technical, e.g. any personal circumstances which prevent you from working on your project
- Take pride in and responsibility for your work; prioritise and organise your work in such a way that it represents your best efforts.

Please note, although your supervisor will point out problems and errors in your written work, he or she will expect you to proofread your own text, and will assume that it represents your best effort. Only then will you be able to maximise the resource that is your supervisor, and thus enhance your own learning during the project. Remember, too, that your supervisor is a busy person with limited time. If you hand in material that is carefully proofread, well structured and clearly written, it means that the supervisor can spend less time on commenting presentation details. As a result, more time can instead be spent on discussing your results, future directions for your work etc. In this way, you will be using your portion of the supervisor's time more efficiently. As a general guideline, it is well worth to keep in mind that it is your project, and under no circumstances should the supervisor do the work for you!

3.1.2 Projects with Multiple Students

When there are multiple students working on the same project, there are additional issues to be taken into account, e.g. project co-ordination and responsibilities. Although larger projects with many people have some unifying problems and goals, it is generally a good idea to identify unique parts of the problem, which can then be assigned to each person. However, in certain situations it is difficult to allocate responsibilities and tasks fairly and evenly among the project members. In these circumstances, it is essential that all project members are held equally responsible for the outcome of the project. It is good for both students and supervisors if students are allocated distinct problems in the project, even when there will be extensive collaboration resulting in one report. In the event of your writing one report together, it is important to realise that you are all equally responsible for its content.

3.2   The Supervisor

The supervisor is a person who is there to guide you, both in the subject area and in scientific thinking. The supervisor is normally skilled in carrying out projects in the particular subject area, and knowledgeable about the methods relevant to and accepted in that subject area.

Your supervisor should help you choose and define the boundaries of the topic to be studied in the project. The supervisor helps you ensure that your project can be completed successfully and on time. This includes setting the project boundaries in such a way that it is of a reasonable size with respect to the allocated time. It should also be of a reasonable level of complexity with respect to the academic degree. Furthermore, the supervisor will help you ensure that there are appropriate literature or data sources available in the area.

Throughout the duration of the project, the supervisor monitors progress by regularly meeting with you in person and discussing the project. It is preferable to complement these meetings with email contact.

One of the most important aspects of a thesis project is that it gives you training in approaching problems in an independent and systematic manner. You are likely to find that your supervisor is a valuable source of reflection, which will stimulate you to critically evaluate and reflect on your own work, as well as that of other people.

3.2.1   The Responsibilities of a Supervisor

Here we give a list of the responsibilities of a supervisor. The list should not be seen as complete, but nevertheless it represents a good set of guidelines concerning the role. The supervisor should:

- Inform you of the instructions of your particular department or university for carrying out a thesis project
- Inform you of assessment criteria and the expected standard of thesis projects
- Discuss dates when your work should be handed in, presented or discussed
- Provide guidelines for how to report the project
- Discuss with you what is expected in terms of how you should work together
- Give guidance concerning the nature of research, the standard expected, relevant literature and sources in the area, and what research methods are considered good practice in the area
- Inform you of relevant regulations and issues, legal as well as ethical, e.g. copyright issues, plagiarism
- Explore your academic background to identify any areas in which further training is required (including, not only knowledge related to the topic of your project, but also language and writing skills)
- Help you ensure that your project can be completed, including preparation of a report, within the allocated project time, and advise you accordingly

- Meet you regularly and discuss the progress in the project (how often depends on the type of project, and what phase the project is in)
- Request that you hand in written reports (or other material, as appropriate for the type of project), within an agreed time
- Inform you of any inadequacy with respect to progress or the quality of the work, or in the worst case, of failure to reach an acceptable standard

Although writing is a continuous process throughout the project, as it gets closer to completion the writing intensifies. The supervisor should provide guidance on your writing and preparation of the report, including commenting on at least one complete draft and the final version of the report before it is submitted (or goes to the printer). However, it is important to stress that the supervisor is not expected to undertake major editing, or revision of a draft report. After all, you are the one responsible for the work done in the project, and the primary responsibilities of the supervisor are to provide advice and guidance to you in your quest for new knowledge.

In reasonable time before completion, the supervisor should ensure that you are prepared for the oral part of the examination, i.e. the defence. This means that you need to understand the role of the oral examination in the overall examination process, be well prepared to present your work, and adequately respond to questions about it. In order to improve your presentation skills and prepare you for the oral examination, the supervisor can help a good deal by arranging opportunities for you to present your work, e.g. at seminars at the department.

After the oral examination, the supervisor should advise and assist you in the preparation of the final manuscript, addressing the implications of any recommendations made by the examiner.

3.2.2 *Projects with Multiple Supervisors*

A project with multiple supervisors requires good working practices for the communication between all the parties involved. It is recommended that one of the supervisors be appointed as primary supervisor, with overall responsibility for supervision of the project. The supervisors should decide between them how best to co-ordinate their supervision; what their roles are with respect to the project, and what they expect to contribute to the supervision of the student.

3.3 The Examiner

The examiner is the person who assesses your project, either continuously or summatively. There are two typical roles an examiner can take. We call these roles *quality evaluator* and *quality assuror*. The examiner's involvement in the process depends on which role he or she takes. In explaining these two roles we stress the important characteristics of each in order to emphasise the differences. Of course, in practice the examiner may combine elements from the two roles.

3.3.1   The Examiner as Quality Evaluator

When evaluating the quality of the work, the examiner focuses on a *result oriented* approach, i.e. the quality of the work based on the contribution made, the complexity of the problem, the usefulness of the solutions and how well presented the work is.

In this approach the examiner is only involved at the very end of the project when the work is close to completion (or has been completed). Hence, the evaluation is based on the report and the oral defence. Furthermore, during the project there is no project-related communication between the examiner and yourself, nor between the examiner and the supervisor. This is the typical scenario for graduate degrees, such as doctoral degrees and also possibly master's degrees.

The advantage of this approach is that the objectivity of the examiner can be maintained more easily, since he or she is not biased by any involvement in earlier phases of the project. The disadvantage is that the examiner cannot assess you with respect to those criteria which are related to your own performance and independence in the process. This is due to the examiner's lack of insight into the process, and how you and your supervisor have been working together. See Fig. 3.2 for an illustration of this. The numbers along the axis represent the number of weeks in an example project.

3.3.2   The Examiner as Quality Assuror

An alternative to just evaluating the quality of the outcome, is that the examiner reviews material produced at different checkpoints in your project. This enables the examiner to gain a deeper understanding of your progress. When this is the case, the examiner normally takes on the responsibility of also assuring the quality. Most importantly, however, the examiner takes on a more *process-oriented view*. In

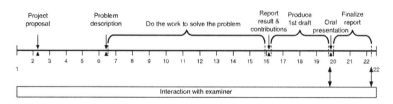

Fig. 3.2 The examiner as quality evaluator

addition to evaluating the results, the examiner monitors and evaluates your progress at certain checkpoints. At these points in time the examiner may give feedback to you and/or your supervisor, which indicate the strengths and weaknesses of your work, possibly together with suggestions which may be of help in addressing any weaknesses. See Fig. 3.3 for an illustration of the process, with checkpoints where the examiner interacts with you and your supervisor.

The advantage of having the examiner involved in earlier phases is that both you and your supervisor can see how an external person perceives the work, since the examiner is not directly involved the project. Furthermore, if the examiner provides regular feedback throughout the project, it is less likely that big issues and concerns will be discovered only at the end. However, the examiner has to be cautious. If the examiner gives feedback during the process, he or she will also affect the final result of the project. This implies that, at the end, the examiner is evaluating the quality of a product, which has been influenced by his or her earlier comments. Hence, it can be argued, justifiably, that there is a risk that the examiner will be less objective when evaluating the final product. The examiner must therefore be very careful about maintaining objectivity. It is much harder for examiners to do this than simply to evaluate the outcome of the project. Feedback during the project, in order to avoid the examiner becoming the supervisor, should generally be kept to a minimum. This approach offers better insight into the process, resulting in a better understanding of how you have matured, and how you have progressed during the project. In fact, you can now be assessed with an additional criterion related to the process, which is not possible when the examiner acts only as a quality evaluator.

At some stages of the project, the examiner may take a more active role in monitoring the process. In the interest of wanting to see as many successful projects as possible, the examiner may offer some assistance during the initial stages of the project. At this stage, the examiner can have a significant positive influence, by giving both you and your supervisor feedback and support during the process of defining the problem area and setting the goals for the project.

The other situation, in which the examiner may take a more active role, is if some problem arises. You may be unhappy with the supervision, or your supervisor may be unhappy with your progress. In such situations, it is advisable to contact the examiner and to ask for his or her advice.

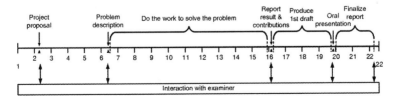

Fig. 3.3 The examiner as quality assuror

3.3.3 The Responsibilities of an Examiner

It is the responsibility of an examiner to scrutinise your work and point out its strengths and weaknesses, as well as to decide if you pass or not and to set your grade. He or she will likely initiate a discussion with you in order to test your ability to reason about the problem and its solutions from alternative perspectives. Test criteria that are commonly used include:

- Level of creativity in the process
- Ability to analyse and reason in different situations
- Clarity in written presentation
- Oral presentation skills and ability to defend the work, i.e. to respond to scrutinising questions
- The relevance and originality of the problem and topic
- How well you are able to separate your own work from the work of others, and how well you are able to manage citations of other work
- How well the project has been managed with respect to time and the project plan

This concludes the first part of the book. In the next part, the process is described in detail.

Part II
Process

4
The Process – An Overview

In this chapter, we present an overview of the process of conducting thesis projects. Briefly, the process consists of seven activities, which are carried out by you. In addition, your supervisor and examiner are involved in four activities, which focus on controlling the quality of your project at different stages. Figure 4.1 presents an overview of the process.

The process starts with an activity in which you develop a project proposal. The project proposal is a short description of your initial ideas about what you would like to do, and how you intend to achieve the overall goal of the project. The project proposal is submitted for quality control.

Once the project proposal has been accepted, the ideas in your proposal are developed into a more extensive problem description. Typically, developing a problem description includes activities such as searching for information at the university library, developing the aim (the overall goal) and objectives (how to reach the aim) of the project, and developing arguments which support the aim. The problem description is then submitted for quality control. It is a common practice to present the problem description at a seminar where, possibly among others, both your examiner and supervisor are present.

You then continue the process by doing the actual work; following the objectives, collecting the data, analysing and presenting it, and drawing conclusions from the results. At this stage, the project is near completion, and a complete first draft of your report can be submitted for quality control. This quality control point can be used by your supervisor and examiner to investigate whether you have made satisfactory progress, before allowing you to present and defend the work at a seminar.

In general, the presentation and defence of your work will provide you with valuable feedback, which is useful for preparing the final version of your report. Finally, your examiner (possibly with assistance from your supervisor) evaluates and grades the submitted thesis.

The process and activities depicted in Fig. 4.1 are explained in detail in the forthcoming chapters.

M. Berndtsson et al. (eds.), *Thesis Projects: A Guide for Students in Computer Science and Information Systems.*
© Springer 2008

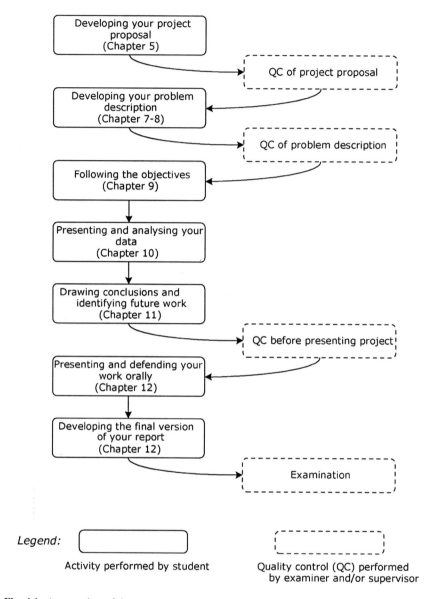

Fig. 4.1 An overview of the process

5
Developing your Project Proposal

A project proposal is a brief description of what you intend to do. Typically, a project proposal is only a few pages long. On these few pages you need to introduce the reader to the:

- *Subject area*. What is the topic and scope of your project?
- *Aim*. What is the goal of your project?
- *Arguments*. Why is it important to investigate the chosen topic?
- *Objectives*. Preliminary ideas for how you intend to achieve the aim.

Figure 5.1 presents an overview of activities to be carried out when developing a project proposal. In subsequent sections, we shall take a closer look at each one of these activities.

5.1 Choosing a Subject Area

As outlined above, the subject area is the topic of your project. Some example areas within computer science and information systems are: electronic commerce, software engineering and human-computer interaction. Apart from choosing a subject area, it is necessary to describe the topic of your project in more detail, for example:

- *Database systems*. Object-oriented databases, relational databases, active databases, multimedia databases, distributed databases, etc
- *Electronic commerce*. Infrastructure, web auctions, web shops, company strategies for implementing electronic commerce, etc
- *Software engineering*. Software testing, object-oriented modelling, CASE tools, rapid prototyping, etc
- Human-computer interaction. Usability, interface design, visualisation, etc

These examples show that the names of subject areas often correspond to course names, titles of textbooks, or keywords in research articles.

M. Berndtsson et al. (eds.), *Thesis Projects: A Guide for Students in Computer Science and Information Systems.*
© Springer 2008

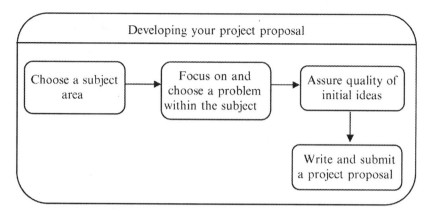

Fig. 5.1 Developing a project proposal

In some situations, a subject area consists of a combination of other subject areas, for example, databases and human-computer interaction. These could be combined, perhaps, to become *user interfaces for database systems*. In addition, there are subject areas that combine computer science or information science with another academic field. For example, bioinformatics can be viewed as a combination of computer science and biology. Although these types of subject areas are worthwhile to explore, it can be problematic to find a supervisor for such a project. The supervisor should know the related subject area well. Alternatively, you may need two supervisors.

5.1.1 Start Early

Finding and choosing a subject area for the project is a task that benefits from being initiated well before the actual project begins. Start thinking about possible subject areas early, and let the decision regarding the chosen area of study be refined incrementally. In this way, you can avoid hastily made decisions that are not well motivated.

Another benefit of starting early is that before the project begins, you may have time to identify and check important sources of information. The time it takes to, for example, identify and order literature or discuss a proposal with a company, should not be underestimated. It is much better to do this before the project starts, than when the project is already underway. This does not mean that you should launch a complete literature analysis before the actual project commences. But you should try to familiarise yourself with the most important sources of information, and investigate whether they will be available when the project begins.

Keep in mind that there are many different sources of information, not only books. Libraries usually have several ways of supplying information. The first and obvious are the library's own literature resources (books, journals etc.), but most libraries will also organise inter-library loans if they do not have the literature you want.

Most libraries provide access to bibliographies and bibliographic databases. These contain large numbers of documents that can be of interest, and which can be searched by author, title, subject and keywords. This is a good way of finding interesting articles from journals and conferences. They often contain information on new subjects and recent research, not yet published in books. Many libraries also have access to full-text databases, where the complete texts of articles (often including figures and tables) are made available. These databases have the advantage of providing access to the articles immediately; a fast and effective way to obtain information. Examples of useful bibliographies are provided in the appendix.

In addition to your library, you may want to search for information on the Internet. Searching for information on a given topic may be difficult – at least if you do not have any good places on the Internet from which to begin. You might try some of the common search engines, although there are likely to be many hits at first. In most situations there will be an overflow of search results, and you might have trouble selecting the relevant information.

You should also find out if your university subscribes to Internet access for journals in your field of study. If so, this could allow you to search those journals' archives of past articles, and to print out any articles that are useful to you.

If you cannot find any literature at the library associated with your subject area, it may be an indication of one of the following:

- Your chosen subject area is too novel for a B.Sc. or M.Sc. project. Your chosen area is more suitable for a Ph.D. project.
- You are looking in the wrong place. Try other sources, such as journals or conference proceedings. Sometimes it may help to use a different set of keywords when searching bibliographic databases.
- You are in the wrong library!

Searching for information is discussed in detail in Chap. 13.

5.1.2 How to Choose a Subject Area

Which subject area to choose is a decision that only you can make; nobody else will make this decision for you.

One of the most crucial factors for succeding with a project is the motivation for undertaking the work in the chosen subject area. You should strive to choose the subject area that you are most interested in. This will have a positive effect on the entire project.

Choose a subject area where you have the necessary skills. Do not choose a subject area in which, for example, you have failed courses.

A combination of areas is usually a good source of interesting problems and topics for project proposals. At the same time, it is not recommended that you choose a project which combines more than two areas, since they can become too complex to handle.

In addition to the above guidelines, ask yourself whether you:

- Have previously in your studies encountered subject areas or courses that you felt were especially interesting
- Would like to work within a particular subject area in the future

5.2 Choose Problem to Focus on Within the Subject Area

Once you have found a subject area for your project, it is time to focus your interests within the chosen area. You focus your interest by identifying a problem within the subject area that you would like to explore. For example, a potential problem within database systems is how to map a logical database design to a physical database design.

You should try to find problems which are of general interest, or which can be generalised or applied, for example, to several companies or organisations.

Here are some ways to identify a problem within the subject area:

- Ask yourself what you would like to do within a particular area (or what you can do, given your current knowledge).
- Read the literature, since others may have already identified and reported the issues that are worthwhile to explore. You may even find that somebody else has already done what you were planning to do. In this situation you can adjust your aim, so that it targets something that other information sources do not cover. It is better to find this out sooner rather than later, since there is no point in reinventing the wheel.
- Ask potential supervisors, as they typically have ideas on what could be worthwhile and interesting to explore within the subject area. Sometimes they will have project proposals already written down. Frequently, project proposals will be in the context of the supervisor's own professional research areas. This may increase the likelihood that he or she will be highly motivated to act as a supervisor for the project.
- Ask companies and organisations, as they may have encountered problems that they do not have time, knowledge or resources to investigate themselves. Such problems or ideas are typically very specific. Hence, you will need to discuss them with a potential supervisor in your department, who should be able to help you put the company's specific problem into a wider context.

Avoid setting up a project in an area in which you do not have the necessary background. Suppose, for example, you have read an interesting article about database design, and you begin thinking about doing a project in this area. If you have not previously studied database systems, then you would have to spend valuable time reading and trying to understand basic concepts. This is not a good way to begin a project, since too much time would be spent reading about the basics of the subject area. It is also much more difficult to identify relevant problems if you are unfamiliar with the area in general.

Once you have found a problem, you need to investigate whether it is worthwhile to explore further. Try to write down your arguments for why it is important to investigate the problem. If you find clues in the existing literature that the problem is still not solved, then you are on the right track. On the other hand, if you find no supporting clues in the literature, you have to develop all the arguments yourself.

Your initial ideas can be further refined by asking yourself – what type of project would I really like to do? Should it be, for example:

- A descriptive project
- A theory oriented project
- An applied project
- A comparison of theory and practice

Keep in mind that most thesis projects use elements from more than one of the above categories. Use the categories to identify the main characteristic of your approach. In the subsequent sections, we take a closer look at each of these project types.

5.2.1 Descriptive Projects

Descriptive projects present the state-of-the art for a given subject. A descriptive project can be set up in different ways. Here we outline two common types of descriptive projects.

In the first type, the aim is to categorise and compare previous work within a subject area. This may include objectives such as (1) categorising previous work, (2) selecting comparison criteria, and (3) comparing previous work with respect to the comparison criteria. This type of survey is useful when you want to identify how a subject area has evolved over time, what its current status is, and how it may evolve in the near future.

In the second type of project, the aim is to gain an understanding of the current status of the subject, and to identify important factors. This may include objectives such as (1) selecting questions, (2) interviewing people, and (3) identifying important factors from the interviews.

When you choose to do a descriptive project, it is important that you do not write a report which is simply a summary of all the literature you have read in the field. Instead you need to, e.g. highlight your analysis of the literature.

5.2.2 Theory Oriented Projects

Theory oriented projects often deal with extending or comparing existing theoretical models without testing them in practice. Here we outline two common types of theoretical projects.

In our first example of a theoretical project, the aim is to extend an already existing theory or model; to extend the relational data model with support for business rules. This may include objectives such as (1) identifying the details of the extension (e.g. what types of business rules), (2) introducing the extension to the original theoretical model, and (3) comparing the original theoretical model with the extended version.

In our second project example, the aim is to compare the support for business rules in two different data models. This project is an example of a comparison between two theoretical models; This may include objectives such as (1) selecting comparison criteria, and (2) analyzing the two data models with respect to the comparison criteria.

When you choose to do a theoretical project, it is important that you are aware of how the theoretical ideas may be applied in practice. Although a theoretical project does not involve implementing or otherwise testing the theory in practice, it is nevertheless important that the theory/model is correct.

5.2.3 Applied Projects

Applied projects often deal with conducting experiments and building proof-of-principle implementations, and gathering experiences from them. Here we outline one common type of applied project.

In this type of applied project, the aim is to gain experience from implementing an algorithm for caching of web data. This may include objectives such as (1) setting up a simulator, (2) implementing the new algorithm, (3) testing and analyzing the results obtained, and (4) suggesting improvements to the algorithm.

An applied project should not be a consulting job. If it were, it would probably satisfy the company where the project is carried out, but in most cases would not meet the requirements of a thesis project. There is a tendency for such projects to be carried out in isolation from the related theory. One way around this is to take a practical problem, e.g. from a company, and put it into a theoretical context. It then becomes easier to demonstrate the importance of investigating the company's problem.

5.2.4 A Comparison of Theory and Practice

Projects which combine theory and practice may contrast the theory with current practice in companies or organisations. Here we outline one example project.

In this example project, the aim is to contrast the current theory relating to object-oriented modelling, with how companies and organisations use object-oriented modelling in practice. This may include objectives such as (1) selecting companies or organisations, (2) selecting comparison criteria, (3) investigating the details of the theory with respect to the comparison criteria, (4) investigating how companies or organisations work with object-oriented modelling with respect to the comparison criteria, and (5) a comparison of the results obtained from (3) and (4).

5.3 Assure Quality of Initial Ideas

Unless you have already discussed your initial project ideas with a potential supervisor, now is the time to do this. A potential supervisor can check your initial project ideas in terms of overall quality.

If you start with a project idea suggested by a supervisor, it is still important to write a project proposal yourself. It is not a good idea to just copy the supervisor's description of the idea, and use that as your project proposal. Your potential supervisor wants to know that you have understood the idea, that you have really thought about the problem yourself, and that you are able to develop the idea further by yourself. Therefore, you must write a project proposal which develops the supervisor's ideas further, expresses your own understanding of that idea and contains your own thoughts of how it can be developed.

5.4 Write and Submit a Project Proposal

Generally, a project proposal is one to a few pages long. However, the recommended length and the level of detail of the project proposal may vary from department to department. You must therefore, check with your department what guidelines they have and what standard they expect. Writing is best begun as soon as you have decided on the subject area.

Once the proposal is finished, you submit it for quality control. Although you may feel that you have not read and understood everything in the problem domain, try to be as clear as possible in your writing. It is important to keep in mind that your reviewer (supervisor or examiner) will view the proposal as coming from you. When the reviewer starts asking difficult questions about the project proposal, you are the one who has to be able to answer those questions. Already at this point in time, the project is considered to be yours and not your supervisor's.

5.4.1 Structure

In this section we present a simple structure for the project proposal (see Fig. 5.2). First, you need to introduce your chosen subject area to the reader. Second, focus

---

Title of project?

Introduction
  - To the subject area (e.g., XML documents).
  - To the problem within the subject area (e.g., preserving links when transforming XML
    documents to another data format).

Reasons why it is important to investigate the chosen problem.

Aim of project
  A short description of what you intend to do.

Objectives
  How (by what steps) do you intend to achieve the aim of the project?

Name
Contact information (email, phone)

Fig. 5.2 An example structure of a project proposal

your interest within the subject area on a specific problem. Having done this, begin developing arguments that back up your aim and objectives. Remember that one of the main purposes of the project proposal is to convince the reader that your project is worthwhile. If you can present good arguments for why it is important for someone to undertake your project, as captured by your stated aim, then you have laid the first brick in planning a solid project. Do not use subjective arguments such as "I would like to do X because I think X is interesting". Your reviewer could then easily reject the project proposal with "I don't think X is interesting". There must instead be objective reasons for why the project needs to be done. Ideally, these reasons originate in the gaps in current knowledge within the subject area.

The project aim is a question or a problem definition within the subject area that you would like to pursue. For example,

To investigate the usage of electronic commerce in small and medium sized companies during the last 10 years.

You should keep in mind that one of the requirements of the project is that it should be *original* to some degree, see Sects. 1.2 and 5.2. Therefore, you should point out in your proposal what particular piece of knowledge is currently missing, and that you aim to provide us with this by doing your project. In addition, you should explain why this piece of knowledge is useful or necessary. For example, how to optimise queries in distributed main memory databases (missing knowledge) would be useful to know, because it would give users faster responses.

The objectives are the means by which to achieve the aim. Usually, they are presented as a list of activities to carry out in order to achieve the aim. See earlier Sects. 5.2.1–5.2.4 for examples of objectives.

If it is possible for you to make your preferences known with regard to the choice of supervisor, here are some guidelines for making the right choice:

- Ask previous students how they were supervised by the person you have in mind.
- Browse theses of students who were supervised in previous years by your potential supervisor.
- Check whether the supervisor will be available or not. Check that your potential supervisor will not be away from office for half of your project. We do not recommend having a supervisor who is too heavily involved in other activities.
- Check how active they are within their research areas. If you have two equally good candidates, it might be advantageous for your project to choose the supervisor who seems to be most active in his or her field. This can be difficult to determine, but one approach is to check the descriptions of research activities on their personal web pages.
- Talk to the potential supervisor. If you have not met before, it might be good to talk to him or her to see whether you have any personal differences.

5.4.2 Project Proposal Checklist

If you submit a well-written project proposal to the reviewer, you can get a head start of your project and probably also avoid time-consuming resubmissions of your proposal.

Before submitting the project proposal to the reviewer, check the following:

- *Proper language.* Is the wording in the project proposal clear and concise?
- *Mandatory information.* Does the project proposal contain the required information?
- *Quality assurance.* Have you discussed the project proposal with a potential supervisor or someone else who has knowledge in the chosen subject area?
- *Skills and resources.* Do you have the necessary background and resources to do a project in the chosen subject area?
- *Time.* Have you estimated the time it takes to complete the project? Preferably, your estimation should also include some slack to cater for any project delays.

After you have submitted the project proposal, continue to read the literature, arrange meetings etc. while you are waiting for a response from the reviewer.

5.5 Quality Control of Project Proposal

A reviewer can get a good overview of the quality of the project proposal very quickly by checking the language, mandatory information etc. In addition, the reviewer will check that your proposed project is not too simple, too advanced, too small, too fuzzy, too broad, too specific or too big. Project proposals that fall into these categories are in most cases a sign that you have not carried out enough quality assurance checks before submitting it. These problems can be resolved in most cases by further discussions with (potential) supervisors and revision of the proposal.

5.6   Matching Supervisors and Students

In this section, we assume that the person responsible for matching supervisors and students is already in dialogue with supervisors. Matching supervisors and students is not as easy as it may seem, and is often constrained by the following factors:

- Availability of supervisors within the subject area. Typically, there are not many potential supervisors within a given subject area in each department. This causes problems when there are many students wanting a particular supervisor and he or she is the only available person with knowledge in a particular subject. For example, suppose that ten students would like to be supervised by a particular person. Unfortunately, since the supervisor will have other commitments and obligations, it may only be possible for him or her to supervise two students at any one time. Thus, only two of the ten students will get their preferred supervisor.
- Availability of supervisors outside the subject area. When asked, students are often reluctant to be supervised by someone who is only vaguely familiar with the subject area. However, this person may have substantial experience of supervising projects. Such a supervisor is often very good at posing the right questions, and thereby helping the student to move the project forward. If possible, an external domain expert may be brought in as co-advisor, and thereby compensate the main supervisor's lack of expertise in the subject area. Therefore, being assigned a supervisor who is only vaguely familiar with the subject area, may not be the disadvantage that it first appears.
- Personal suitability of supervisors. In some situations, the supervisor may have a connection with the student, with the implication that he or she may not be a suitable supervisor for that student. For example, the potential supervisor may be a close friend of the student. In this particular case, it can be difficult for the supervisor to distinguish between the two roles: friend versus supervisor. Alternatively, personal differences between the supervisor and student may make the supervisor unsuitable.

Given the above factors it is impossible, in practice, to satisfy all students' wishes concerning a preferred supervisor. Some students will be assigned the supervisor they wanted; but some will be assigned a supervisor who was not on their list. In most situations, this will still be all right. However, the person responsible for assigning supervisors to projects should also be sensible enough to detect situations where the match of student and supervisor is not going to work.

6
References and Citations

When developing the project proposal, you should refresh your knowledge of how to identify appropriate literature and how to use citations.

6.1   Appropriate References

A reference is a description that identifies an information source. For example, the following reference describes a (fictional) journal article written by K. Anderson:

Anderson, K. (2008). The Untold Story of Computer Science. *International Journal of Computer Science*, 2(1), 23–35.[1]

By properly referencing the material your work is based upon, you achieve several things. You:

- Show how your work extends the current state-of-the-art knowledge in the area
- Show the originality of your work
- Give credit to other people's work (and thereby avoid being accused of plagiarism)
- Support and validate arguments made in your report (any claim made in the report must be supported either by your own research or by citing results published by other people)
- Show that you are familiar with the work done in the area

By simply looking at your reference list, an experienced reader or reviewer will see whether you have used references from well known sources, or sources that are not of such good quality. Furthermore, you can strengthen your arguments in the report if you base them on well known references which have been published in high-quality scientific journals, or in proceedings from renowned conferences.

Another reason why references are needed is to make your work reproducible. Anyone who reads your report should be able to reproduce your work, and therefore

---

[1] Details concerning the information (e.g., volume number, page number) contained in the reference are given in Chapter 14.6.

M. Berndtsson et al. (eds.), *Thesis Projects: A Guide for Students in Computer Science and Information Systems*.
© Springer 2008

all sources you have used must be clearly identified. This is especially important if your work is an extension of an existing solution, method or theory. If the reader cannot find the literature containing the original work, then they cannot verify that your extension is based on a correct interpretation of the original solution, method or theory.

A reference is judged to be appropriate for your work, depending on its content and its type. You can check the relevance of a reference's content by considering removing the reference from your text. If you cannot remove the reference without losing essential information then the reference should be kept, otherwise it can be removed.

There are different types of documents that you can use as references:

- Scientific research journals typically publish high quality articles. These articles are written by experts in the field for other experts, which may make them difficult to understand for non-experts. In many cases one or more conference and workshop articles precede the journal article. Consequently, the work reported in the journal may be of high quality, but the research findings may have become somewhat outdated. Therefore, it is always good to check whether the article provides information on when it was first submitted.
- Conference and workshop proceedings publish quality papers relatively fast (compared with most journals). If possible, check the acceptance ratio, i.e. the number of accepted papers divided by the number of submitted papers. Conferences and workshops with a low acceptance ratio, e.g. 15–30%, are likely to have very good papers, whereas the quality of papers at a conference with a high acceptance ratio (say 80–85%) can be questionable. Try to identify which conferences and workshops within your area have good reputations. Your supervisor can probably give you guidance concerning this.
- Theses (M.Sc., Ph.D.) contain valuable information which, to a varying degree, present the state of the art for a subject. As theses are examined and assessed, they are usually of adequate quality. A Ph.D. thesis presents research results that someone has been working on for 3 years or more, and a M.Sc. thesis is the result of half a year of research. Thus, you can expect that the material in a Ph. D. thesis is of higher quality and more extensive than similar material in a M.Sc. thesis.
- Textbooks are usually a good source for understanding the fundamentals in a variety of subjects and areas. These books are frequently used in courses. In general, textbooks are reviewed but they do not cover the latest research findings, since they are mainly used for teaching established knowledge. New findings take some years to become established, and are therefore not included in most textbooks until some years have passed. However, there are also some textbooks that cover advanced issues and the latest research findings. These advanced textbooks are typically aimed at researchers and Ph.D. students.
- Magazines can be viewed as a popular version of research journals. Some articles published in magazines may be reviewed, while others may not be. Even if some magazines contain articles on research results, it is usually only in the form

of summaries and often with simplifications, to make the material more accessible to non-experts. If such an article contains a reference to a an article in a reseach journal, then you should always try to find the original source. When reading magazines that are published by companies that, e.g. sell a particular computer program, you should be aware that articles in these magazines will probably not criticise products or statements of the company.

- Web pages can contain useful information, but in general, they should be avoided since their content is normally not reviewed. Moreover, they can quickly disappear or change. In some cases the research information on a web page will have been published at a conference or in a journal also. In this case, you should obtain the article or conference paper and make your reference to the original source. Do not use the web URL as reference in such cases.

- Newspapers can provide interesting pieces of information, which you can use as examples in your report. However, it is not good to base the report heavily on references to articles that have appeared in newspapers, since you normally do not know whether the article has been reviewed by an expert in the field. In addition, articles in newspapers do not present all the details that you need for your project. For example, you may find an article in a newspaper that describes a robot that is able to play soccer. The article will probably present an overview of what the robot can do, but it will probably not present any details concerning the algorithms for playing soccer or what the software architecture looks like. These details are probably published in research journals or in the proceedings of research conferences. If you use any newspaper articles, look for names of researchers, or names of institutions. These names can help you locate the corresponding research publications.

- Other documents such as manuals, modelling documents, and commercial information should also be treated with care. In general, these documents are not reviewed, and hence there is no guarantee that they are of good quality. Moreover, documents published by companies may be written in such a way that they advertise the company's products, rather than presenting neutral facts.

In general, a written document is of better quality than an oral statement. The reason is simple; one can always go back to a written document and check the exact details of it, whereas an oral source may have forgotten some details over time. In addition, the material in a written source will usually have been reviewed before it was printed.

Do not use oral sources as the main argument in your project aim, since this will reduce the trustworthiness of your arguments. Instead, if you need to include some oral sources when you describe the project aim and its arguments, you should do so in combination with literature sources. In the next two paragraphs we outline two situations when it is appropriate to use oral sources in conjunction with a literature source.

Suppose that you use information from a research article as one of the major arguments for your project aim. If you have been in contact with the authors of this research article, and they gave you additional oral information, for example, on how they reached a certain result, then you can refer to this oral source. It will enhance the reader's understanding of the research article.

Similarly, oral statements can be used together with a literature source in order to describe real life situations. For example, if you have a research article on database security, you can use oral references (or newspaper articles) in order to describe situations which occurred when database security was low.

6.2   Citations

A citation is the use of a reference in the text. For example, the two following citations highlight that the journal article by K. Anderson describes four areas for future research.

Anderson (2008) describes four areas for future research ...
There are four main areas for future research (Anderson, 2008).

The main reason why citations to references should be used in your report, is to distinguish clearly between your own work and that of others. It is a good idea to keep the following rule in mind while writing:

Everything in your report that does not come with a citation will be assumed to be your own work.

In other words, if you state a fact in your report, your supervisor will assume that you have discovered that fact yourself, unless you provide a citation to a reference showing where you have read it.

It is the responsibility of the author to justify and verify statements that have no citations to references. You should make it clear at all times when the material is not your own. This does not necessarily mean that every sentence should have a citation, but paying too little attention to citations can endanger your entire project. For example, in the examination you will be asked to defend and justify statements in the report which have no associated reference. You may find this difficult if you are unaware of the details of the underlying argument. Furthermore, your examiner or supervisor may be familiar with the statement in its original context, and they will then know that you have incorrectly claimed it as your own work.

Citations in the text follow several rules. According to The Chicago Manual of Style (1993, pp. 644–645) a text citation can be placed

- Before a punctuation mark:
  The human brain contains approximately 50 billion neurons (Smith, 1994).
- At a logical place in a sentence:

According to some researchers (Smith, 1994) there are 50 billion neurons in the human brain.

- At a grammatically correct place in a sentence:
  According to Smith (1994), there are 50 billion neurons in the human brain.
In addition, we recommend that the citation be placed

- Before a list of items

There are five categories of users (Anderson, 2008): (1) students, (2) teachers, (3) professors, (4) technical staff, (5) administrative staff.

When the reference is placed just before the enumerated list, it becomes very clear that the list is taken from something Anderson published in 2008.

- Following quotations

"In the experiments it is shown that the human brain has 50 billion neurons. Many of the types of neurons have yet to be classified. We strongly encourage other researchers to develop tools and techniques that will assist the process of categorising the neurons." (Smith, 1994, p. 345)

A common *mistake* is to place the citation after the last sentence of a paragraph. For example:

Recent work has reported that the importance of computers in industry cannot be overestimated. Several useful services (such as booking train tickets) rely on computers. However, the importance of using computers in our everyday life has been questioned. It has been argued that having too many computers in our everyday life causes security problems, since people cannot protect their computers from hackers and Internet viruses. The researchers are still debating these hot topics. (Jones, 1993)

In this case, the placement of the citation may be intended to imply that it is related to the entire paragraph, since the citation is placed after the last sentence of the paragraph. This style of placement of citations can be very confusing for the reader. For example, suppose that there are five paragraphs on a page, while there is only one citation, which is placed at the end of the last paragraph. It will then be unclear to the reader whether the citation is associated with all the paragraphs (because it is the only citation on the page) or only with the last paragraph. This confusion arises from the fact that citations do not have a specific scope, i.e. the placement of the citation in itself does not tell us how much of the text is related to it. Instead, the author has to carefully choose the placement of the citation, in combination with a choice of wording, in such a way that the reader will be likely to make the correct assumptions.

Here is a further example of how citations may be made in the text, and how they can be improved:

For a long time, the best stock market predictions have been achieved by the Epsilon neural network architecture (Myers and Sang, 1997, Niven, 1999).

In this case, Myers and Sang could be either the developers of the Epsilon architecture, or researchers who have systematically evaluated all stock market prediction programs. In order to clarify this, a better way of citing would be:

The Epsilon neural network architecture, proposed by Myers and Sang (1997), has for a long time been the most accurate method for stock market prediction (Niven, 1999).

It should then be clear to the reader that Myers and Sang developed the particular architecture, wheras Niven evaluated and compared different architectures.

When you have used material from the World Wide Web it is often not necessary to cite the URL of the site or page. For instance, when the URL refers to an online database of scientific data, there is often a published article or paper, which describes the database. The reference can then be made as in the following example:

Example profiles were collected from the HSSP database[2] (Schneider et al., 1997).

The cited paper by Schneider et al. is here a journal article describing the HSSP database. We recommend that the URL be placed either as a footnote, as in this example, or in a list of URL:s that is made separately from the bibliography. Stating the URL in the text is generally not a good idea, unless the address is sufficiently short to not disturb the reading.

In Chap. 14 we describe different reference styles in more detail, as well as what to think about when structuring your report.

6.3   Improve your Learning (and Grade)

Searching for appropriate references can be both rewarding and frustrating. However, what is probably unknown for many students is that the underpinning views you have on information seeking affect your learning.

Briefly, you can approach your information seeking activity with one of the following views:

- That the main reason for information seeking is to find facts that can be used in the thesis.
- That the main reason for information seeking is to evaluate and analyze previous work.

A major study in the field of information seeking and learning showed that those students that had a mere fact finding approach gave evidence of less qualified study results than those who perceived information seeking as a way of evaluating and analyzing a complex issue (Limberg, 2000). Thus, if you use an "evaluate and analyze" approach instead of a "fact finding" approach, you might lay the foundation for a better grade for your thesis.

To evaluate and analyze a complex issue could for example mean that:

- You find information from a variety of sources that provides you with different perspectives on the topic, placing it in a wider context
- You are able to scrutinize information in such a way that you can reveal and structure underlying values and motives in information sources. This can be valuable if you try to find out *how* a particular problem has been investigated or researched by others, rather than just the fact that it has been researched. To widen the perspective and also include the process that has led to these results can often be worthwhile and increase the understanding of a topic

---

[2] Available at URL http://www.sander.embl-heidelberg.de/hssp/

Let us illustrate the above by a short scenario in which you take a first step towards finding information for your thesis project.

Many students would probably immediately claim that the quickest way to find information is to use search engines like Google. Search engines for the Web are very often brilliant tools for finding information, and it certainly can be a good choice for those who are looking for computer-science related information. However, it might be problematic if one expects to find everything that is needed with help of a search engine, since researchers disseminate their research articles through the channels of scientific journals and conferences. These articles might be freely available via the Web, but very often they are not, which means that you might succeed in finding references to documents via a search engine, but you will not be able to access the actual documents. In addition, the documents you find might be drafts, and thus different from the ones that were officially published.

So, if you can not find the appropriate documents with the help of a search engine, then you should investigate the bibliographic databases that are available via the university library. These bibliographic databases are usually available via web interfaces.

Each bibliographic database contains a great number of references to various documents. These documents may have been published in various circumstances and contexts. For instance you will probably find numerous references to articles published in a wide array of different journals, but also to papers published in connection to different conferences; the latter will most likely be labelled as conference proceedings in the database. The problem you now have is to decide what to go for, so to speak. What is the difference between a conference paper and a journal article; is one of them "better" than the other? Could the articles in one particular journal be of higher value than those from another journal? How do you know if a particular author is highly acclaimed within this domain? And what about the authors' affiliations; is it reasonable to believe that a paper written by an author from one particular university is of higher quality than the paper written by an author from another? To be able to answer these kinds of questions it is necessary with practice and experience.

Hopefully our little example scenario shows that it is important to pay attention to such things as the name of the journal (or the conference proceedings) the article was published in – do you have reasons to come back to this journal? – to who the author is – has he or she written more about the subject? – to the details about affiliation – could it be so that the author is a member of a research group in which other documents have been produced that perhaps can be of interest to me? (Here is a good example of when a search engine is an excellent tool, i.e. to identify and locate people). It can also be of importance to note if there is a connection between the kind of articles or papers one can find and the database in which one has found them. If one would try to label these kinds of issues that we have dealt with so far, one could use the term contextual aspects. Unfortunately contextual aspects often tend to be neglected when a novice information seeker conceptualizes information seeking.

Even though these contextual aspects are important it is of course essential to remember that the actual text itself is the main object of evaluation when judging the value of an article. An article written by an unknown author from a university of unknown standards could be equally as good as a n article written by a famous profile within a particular field. There are certain questions that should never be ignored: is the text logically coherent, are the arguments well grounded? Is the text methodologically sound? Are data analyzed in a relevant and correct way? Is there a reasonable correlation between results and conclusions?

The issue of information seeking is discussed in additional detail in Chap. 13.

7
Developing your Aim

To succeed with your project, you first have to define the aim of the project clearly. This is necessary because it clarifies in your own mind exactly what it is you are aiming to achieve. It also helps you to communicate with your supervisor, your examiner and other people whom you want to talk with about your project. To keep the discussions "on track", it is necessary that both you and the person you talk to understand precisely what the project is all about.

Furthermore, the aim is necessary in order to evaluate the usefulness of your project. If you have a clear aim, anyone to whom you present your intended project to can easily judge whether they are interested in the outcome or not.

Finally, formulating a clear statement of the aim at the beginning of your project facilitates evaluation of the outcome when you have completed it. As part of the evaluation, your examiner will check to see if you have fulfilled the aim of your project. Consequently, the activity of developing the aim at the very beginning is a way of finding out what demands your supervisor and examiner will make on a successful project.

Therefore, once your project proposal has been accepted, you should contact your supervisor as soon as possible, in order to discuss necessary refinements to your aim.

7.1 Meetings with Your Supervisor

Meetings with your supervisor are stimulating events where knowledge is created!

The meetings with your supervisor are opportunities for you to present your ideas, get valuable feedback on those ideas, and to discuss all aspects of your project.

At all meetings, it is important that you use the time well. This means that you should come properly prepared, for example by having written down in advance the questions that you would like to ask your supervisor.

The focus of the first meeting with your supervisor will be a discussion regarding what the aim of the project should be. The submitted (and now accepted) project proposal, possibly together with comments from the examiner, represents

45

M. Berndtsson et al. (eds.), *Thesis Projects: A Guide for Students in Computer Science and Information Systems.*
© Springer 2008

input to this first discussion. At the first meeting, we recommend that you agree with your supervisor on how you would like to work together during the project:

- When should meetings take place? We recommend that meetings take place regularly. You might for example, schedule to meet weekly for 1 h. The frequency and length of meetings may depend on a guideline used at your department, or it may be up to the supervisor to decide according to his or her own schedule. If there is a local guideline, the frequency and length of meetings vary a lot between departments. Regardless, it is important to find out how often you will be able to meet your supervisor and to come well prepared to all meetings.
- How and when should material be handed in for comments? Make arrangements for how (e.g. by email or hard copy) and when (e.g. 3 days before the meeting) to hand in material to your supervisor. If you would like your supervisor to read and comment on something that you have written, then you normally need to hand it in at least a couple of days in advance. Otherwise, it is unlikely that your supervisor will have time to read and comment on the text before your meeting. The details of your arrangement depend on the supervisor's schedule and on yours, and this should be agreed upon during the first meeting.

At every meeting it is important that you take the initiative in the discussion, since your supervisor is not the one who should do all the creative thinking in your project. You should not simply ask your supervisor what you should do next. Instead, it is important that you have ideas of your own on what to do. Your supervisor can then give feedback on those ideas.

7.2 Time Plan

The purpose of developing a time plan for your project is for you to have a clear understanding of the relationship between important dates, project activities, and the time needed for each activity. A good time plan helps you to avoid future problems, such as missed deadlines.

When you start your project, your supervisor and examiner will probably already have informed you of a number of important dates. These may be, for example:

- Dates for submission of drafts
- Date for submission of first complete draft
- Date of oral presentation
- Date for submission of final report

These dates are the milestones of your project. Enter these dates into a time plan, preferably by using a computer-based tool. Once you have entered the most important dates in your time plan, you can start to add project activities, how much time you plan to spend on each activity, and the relationship (e.g. overlapping, sequential) between the activities. When you develop the first version of the time plan, you will probably not know all the activities you will need to carry out. This is still all right; you can later refine a broadly described activity, such as *follow objectives*, into a set of specific activities once you have developed the objectives of the project.

As your project progresses, you can enter into the time plan a number of more specific project activities such as:

- Dates for preparation of oral presentation
- Dates for preparation of draft chapters
- Dates for completion of phases or objectives
- Dates for meetings with supervisor

The difficult part with developing a time plan is to accurately estimate the time required for each activity. Thus, it is important that you continuously update your time plan and discuss it with your supervisor for feedback.

Your time plan can be managed and visualised by using different types of diagrams, such as activity networks or Gantt charts. Your university library will probably have books with additional details about these types of diagrams, as well as about project planning in general.

7.3 Activities to Perform While Developing the Aim

Figure 7.1 presents an overview of activities that you need to perform when developing the aim of your project. These activities do not need to be performed in any particular order. Depending on the literature you used when writing your project proposal, you may perhaps be able to refine the aim, write an overall introduction, and develop the arguments behind the project aim by using that literature. In most cases, however, developing the project aim will mean that you need additional literature to support the motivations behind the aim of the project, which

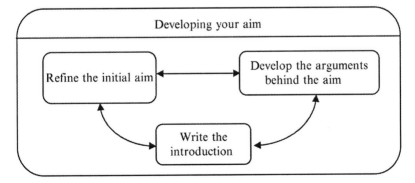

Fig. 7.1 Activities to perform when developing the aim

means in turn that you probably should start searching for additional literature first. In the following sections, we elaborate on each of these activities.

7.3.1 Refine the Initial Aim

Briefly, the aim is a short statement in the form of a clear, unambiguous sentence describing the overall goal of your project. You probably already have a preliminary version of your aim in the project proposal that you submitted earlier. Although the aim itself does not consist of many words, it can be problematic to find the right wording. It is now time to refine the aim into a clear and solid description of your project's goal.

Suppose that you are doing a project related to electronic commerce. Below are three different examples of how the first draft of your aim may look. These example aims are refined later in this section.

Aim 1:   Develop an infrastructure for electronic commerce
Aim 2:   Investigate security issues for electronic commerce
Aim 3:   Investigate the use of electronic commerce for product marketing

It is important that you check and evaluate every word of the aim. Including:

- Are all words clear, or can some words be interpreted to mean different things? If some words can be interpreted in different ways, then readers are likely to misunderstand what you are trying to do. Moreover, you may even become unsure yourself, later in the project, what your aim is really saying.
- Does your aim promise too much? Try to find the right level, so that the aim of the project does not become too simple or too difficult. A project that runs over 6 months and a project that runs over 12 months should not have the same aim. Will you be able to accomplish what you have promised in the aim within the allowed time frame of the project?
- Are there any restrictions on the aim, for example, with respect to area, region, or time periods? A common mistake is to allow time constraints to restrict the project. For example, "due to time constraints in this project, concept X is not investigated". Is this a valid restriction, or is it really a sign that the aim is too ambitious with respect to the allowed time frame for the project?
- Have you explained all the concepts that are used in the aim clearly? All important concepts mentioned in the aim should be defined or explained early in the text.

By considering the above guidelines we could now refine the three example aims mentioned above into:

Aim 1:   Develop a security infrastructure for electronic commerce based on XML

We have here added details concerning the type of infrastructure (security) and that the infrastructure should be based on XML.

Aim 2:   Investigate security issues in negotiation protocols for electronic
          commerce

We have here added details to show that the project is explicitly targeting
security issues for negotiation protocols.

Aim 3:   Investigate the usage of electronic commerce for product marketing by
          small and medium sized companies

We have here added details concerning the size of companies that we are
interested in.

Alternative aim 3:   Investigate the usage of electronic commerce in for product
                      marketing by small and medium sized companies in Sweden
                      and U.S.A.

We have here refined the aim further by adding two countries that we are interested
in studying.

As a test for whether you have formulated your aim well enough, think about
whether you can give a clear answer in two or three sentences if anyone asks: "So
what is your project all about?" You are actually likely to get such questions from
friends and relatives, and you should view such questions as opportunities for
practising, and for seeing if you have a clear understanding of your own project. If
you have difficulties explaining the aim to people who are unfamiliar with the area,
you should think about whether your own understanding of the project is clear
enough, or whether the aim needs further refinement.

7.3.2   Develop the Arguments Behind the Aim

The project aim needs to be supported by proper arguments which explain why it
is important to investigate the topic.

Figure 7.2 shows that your aim can be supported by a number of arguments that
either directly (argument 3 and 4) or indirectly (argument 1 and 2) contribute to

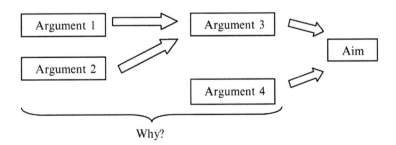

Fig. 7.2   Arguments behind the aim

explaining *why* you are doing the study that is outlined in the aim. The arguments should relate to relevant theory and should have clear links to the aim. For example, consider one of our previous example aims:

> Investigate the usage of electronic commerce in for product marketing by small and medium sized companies in Sweden and U.S.A.

In order to convince the reader that it is worthwhile to pursue this aim, you need to outline the motivation underpinning the aim. First, you need to outline the reasons for why you have chosen electronic commerce. You could do this by explaining that electronic commerce is an interesting area that most companies need to consider, and that lessons can be learned from early attempts to implement such systems. Second, you need to explain why you are focusing on small and medium sized companies. Perhaps it is interesting to focus on these companies since most of them do not have the in-house knowledge on how to implement electronic commerce. Finally, why is it important to study attempts made in Sweden and U.S.A.? One reason may be that you have read reports that from the 1990s that concluded that companies in both countires were at the same level. You could then argue that it would be interesting to investigate whether that situation has changed.

You can add weight to the significance of your aim if you include citations to appropriate[3] references supporting your arguments. For example, if you find a well-argued supporting claim in a scientific journal article or conference paper, then use it. You can then show in your text that somebody else also believes that it is, for example, important to investigate the usage of early electronic commerce systems (provided, of course, that the cited paper provides good arguments for this claim). Be cautious of motives that rely only upon statements of requirements from companies, oral sources, or statements that are not based on sound arguments. As we discussed earlier, the quality of these sources may be questioned.

Using literature to support the aim is an efficient way of strengthening your arguments. Figure 7.3 describes one approach to how to start identifying the literature that may support your aim. First, find important concepts or factors in the aim or in the arguments. Then, find the appropriate literature for these concepts and factors.

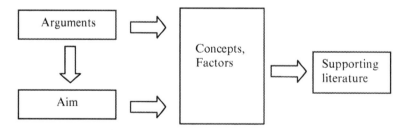

Fig. 7.3 How to identify supporting literature

---

[3] See Chapter 6.1 for an explanation of what is meant by "appropriate" references.

Get to the bones of your chosen subject area, read background material, and the latest research reports in order to establish your own understanding of the core concepts and interpretation of what the state of the art is. For example, a project on the overlap between visualisation and database systems is likely to require a proper explanation of what is meant by "visualisation" and "database systems". Then ask yourself, is there any related work, i.e. has someone else done work similar to that which you are planning? If yes, then it should be described, and the differences between that work and your own project should be pointed out.

You should try to go beyond the textbooks that you have used in your previous courses. Try to read other textbooks or research papers. It is not a good idea to simply use lecture material, e.g. hand-written notes or slides as the main literature source since these contain very limited information.

Figure 7.4 illustrates the literature you might use when developing your aim, and shows how the work described in that literature relates to your project. The chequered box represents the project you are planning to do (or, more precisely, the report you will write as the outcome of your project). The boxes *b*, *c*, and *e* represent literature that describes work that you are directly using in your project. This may be because, for instance, *b* presents an incomplete but promising solution to the problem you are addressing, and you are extending the incomplete solution from *b* with additional features in your solution. Perhaps *c* and *e* contain additional ideas that are directly useful in your work, and they can therefore be considered as giving direct input to your work. These references can be considered as related work, or previous work, which must be cited in your report. When developing the motivations for the aim of your project, you should in this example include a description of why you consider *b* to be an incomplete solution, and why your idea for how to extend *b* is promising.

Literature such as *a* and *d* in Fig. 7.4 may contain necessary background for your aim. Perhaps *a* was the first work to address the particular problem, so that much of your problem description can be based on *a*. The author of *b* may also have

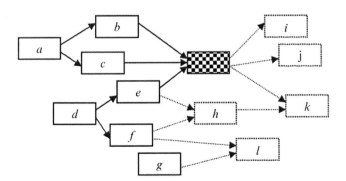

Fig. 7.4 Overview of how your project (chequered box) relates to literature on previous work (*a–g*) and future work (*h–l*)

omitted or misinterpreted something from *a*, which you may then point out in your report. The authors of *d* and *g* may have, independently of *a*, addressed the same problem at a slightly later stage, and would therefore contain additional background to the problem you are addressing.

Although this is the subject of later chapters in this book, it is useful at the beginning of your project to think about how it may relate to future developments in the subject area. Authors of future literature, represented by *i–l* in Fig. 7.4, may cite your work, as well as alternative work that may be taking place simultaneously (such as *h*). Just as you depended on the citations in *b*, *c* and *e* to identify *a* and *d*, it is your duty to provide clear citations and references in your report, which can be used by the future authors of *h–l*. In other words, you should think of your work as being part of the general progression of the area, and keep in mind that for this progression to continue, it is necessary to be able to trace all sources on which a particular piece of work is based.

As you develop the motivations behind the aim, you may find that you need to adjust the wording of the aim. This is a normal process as your knowledge of the details of your chosen problem and subject area increases. Bear in mind that you should always discuss suggestions for refinements of the aim with your supervisor.

When developing the motivations it is important that there should be a clear link between the motivations and the aim. Having read your motivations, the reader should see that there is an obvious need to perform what is specified in the aim. The reader should not have to guess how to link the motivations and the aim. If the motivations are clearly articulated and lead smoothly to the aim, the reader will not be forced to guess how to establish a connection.

7.3.3   Write the Introduction

Once you have started to refine the wording of the aim and its motivations, and identified the appropriate literature, it can be beneficial to develop a high level perspective on your work. The high level perspective serves two purposes. First, it will help the reader to get an overview of your chosen subject area, the identified problems and the aim of the project. Second, it will help you to see the overall picture of your project. In your work you will probably have come across a number of different concepts in the related literature. By taking a high level perspective it becomes possible to see how the various concepts are related to each other and to the aim.

Typically, the first chapter in your report is written as a high level introduction, where you introduce the work and present the overall picture. Briefly you have three building blocks: (1) important concepts and factors (2) motivations behind the aim and (3) the aim. Your task is now to take these three building blocks and investigate how they are related to each other. You can get additional help by looking at

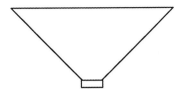
Subject area
Sub-area
Problem
Aspect of problem
Aim

Fig. 7.5 Structure of introductory chapters

the project proposal you submitted earlier. Perhaps you can use the project proposal as a starting point. At this early stage in the project, you should not worry too much about finding the correct wording of the high level introduction. In most situations, it is not until just before you make the final submission of the whole report that you find the correct wording.

Introductory chapters are sometimes written so that they resemble a funnel (Fig. 7.5), i.e. it begins by being quite broad and thereby identifies the whole subject area in which you are doing your project. The funnel then gets narrower by placing your project within a sub-area. Within this sub-area you then identify certain problems which you will address in your project, and select the particular problem (or aspect of the problem) which you will focus on. At this narrow end of the funnel you define your aim. Anyone reading the introductory chapter of your report will then be guided towards a gradually more detailed understanding of how the problem you worked on fits into the subject area.

Additional guidelines for writing the first chapter can be found in Sect. 14.4.3.

8
Developing your Objectives and Choosing Methods

Once you have developed your project aim, you can start to develop objectives, and later also choose a method for each objective. This means that you will shift your focus from what you intend to do (i.e. your aim) to how you intend to structure your work (i.e. your objectives and chosen methods) in order to achieve the aim. For this you can use a four-step process: (1) develop objectives, (2) find potential methods, (3) choose methods, and iv) present details of the chosen set of methods.

This chapter will elaborate both on important concepts and on how you can develop your objectives and choose appropriate methods.

8.1   Important Concepts

Once you have developed your project aim you can start to develop objectives, and later also choose a method for each objective. Figure 8.1 depicts the relationship between your aim, objectives and methods. Your project has one overall aim. In order to reach the aim, a number of objectives are formulated. Each *objective* is a small, achievable and assessable unit, i.e. a sub-goal of the project. Objectives should be formulated in such a way that fulfilling the objectives leads to the overall aim being satisfied.

Each objective can be achieved by different methods. In general terms, by a *method* we refer to a systematic endeavour to address a problem. In addressing a project's aim and its associated set of objectives, you need to identify, for each objective, an appropriate method by which it may be reached. This does not mean that you need to use the same method for addressing all your objectives. Rather, you might want to choose different methods for different objectives. However, in a project which makes use of a combination of methods, the issue of validity becomes more complex. Your choice of methods will have an impact on both the quality of the resulting data and the conclusions you can draw with respect to the overall aim.

Let us now describe the relationship between the aim, objectives and methods by means of a simple analogy. Suppose that you have a green car and you would

M. Berndtsson et al. (eds.), *Thesis Projects: A Guide for Students in Computer Science and Information Systems.*
© Springer 2008

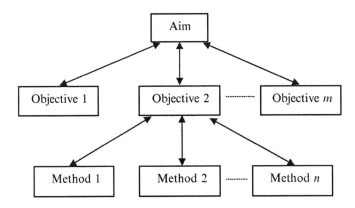

Fig. 8.1 The relationship between aim, objectives and methods

like to change the colour of your car to red. For this project, we can identify *"change colour of car to red"* as the aim of the project. Given the aim, we can formulate a number of objectives as sub-goals:

- Remove parts that should not be painted
- Buy paint
- Paint car
- Re-assemble removed parts once the paint is dry

The activities associated with some of the objectives need to be performed in a sequence (e.g. buying paint followed by painting the car), whereas other objectives do not need to be addressed in a sequence (e.g. removing parts that should not be painted and buying paint can be done in any order).

Let us consider the objective: *"Paint car"*. There are different methods we can apply for painting the car. For example, you can paint your car by:

1. Using an ordinary paintbrush
2. Using a roller
3. Using an airbrush tool
4. Paying the neighbour's son to do the job

All four alternatives can be considered as suitable methods for painting. However, the result will be different in each case. Most likely, method number three will produce the best results with respect to quality. Method number one will change the colour of your car, but the finish will probably be of poor quality. Method number four is probably the one with the most uncertain outcome, where the quality of the result is very difficult to predict.

As in this simple car-painting example, project results can be of poor or good quality, depending on which methods you choose, and how well you are able to use the chosen method.

8.2   Addressing Validity and Reliability

When you are in the process of developing objectives and choosing methods, you should consider how the issues of validity and reliability might affect your project. Briefly, *validity* is the relationship between what you intend to measure (or examine, or develop) and what you actually measure (or examine, or develop). *Reliability* is the accuracy of your method (e.g. implementation, questionnaire, interview style) in measuring (or examining, or developing), i.e. how robust your method is.

A method is only valid and reliable within a certain range of uses. For example, suppose you have a tape measure. This tool is excellent for measuring how tall you are (high validity), but it is not useful for measuring the height of Mount Everest (low validity). Similarly, a tape measure is not particularly reliable, since stretching of the tape, which is somewhat elastic, can result in inaccurate measurements. In comparison, a steel ruler would be more reliable, since it is more rigid and can not be stretched. Thus, a method that you choose to use in your project is only valid and reliable within a certain range of uses.

If you consider validity and reliability issues when you make your choices, with regard to your objectives and methods, you will lay a solid foundation for what you can do in the later stages of your project, for example when presenting and analysing your data. Thereby, you will also improve the overall quality of your project.

We continue our discussion by looking at two important threats to validity which are of particular concern in qualitative research.

The first threat to validity relates to an inability to account for *your bias*. For example, if you are doing a project in an organisation, it is inevitable that you will act on the basis of certain pre-conceptions, a priori theories/views and values that will influence your thinking when undertaking the study. Such influences will, at least to some extent, affect your actions and behaviour during the study. Hence, this will "colour" the way in which you perceive, observe and interpret things in the study. In accounting for this, a comprehensive description of your background and basis is very important when undertaking and reporting the study. Hence, it is important that you account for your own bias, so that, for example, you do not choose an organisational context, or undertake data collection, in such a way that you use it to justify your own pre-conceptions.

Another potential threat to validity relates to *your influence* on the setting under study. For example, in a project that involves participation and data collection by means of interviews, you must account for any situations and circumstances which change during the project. Some changes are subtle and not easily observed, but are nevertheless of fundamental importance when addressing validity. Tacit and subtle changes of this kind include social and human aspects of the phenomena under study, and these are often more difficult to recognise. When doing a series of interviews, it is natural that interviewees should change their views on certain issues; perhaps simply because they have learnt new things due to your project being done in their organisation. In order to minimise this type of threat, you must be aware that any study always influences the organisation to some extent.

Furthermore, if you return later on in the project to the same interviewee for an additional session, you should be aware that the interviewee may now view things differently. In general, it is difficult to completely "identify" and account specifically for individual influences. However, it is important that you understand, and are sensitive to any such change which may occur during your study. We could even say that acknowledging the existence of influences, and having a comprehensive understanding of what is going on in a setting, are prerequisites for accounting for and successfully addressing any potential threats to validity.

You could perhaps argue that it would be desirable to try to eliminate all preconceptions. However, amongst qualitative researchers, it is generally acknowledged that the benefits of "rich data" gained from close observation and interpretation by the researcher are of paramount importance. Therefore, a more fruitful way to proceed is to acknowledge the existence of bias, and to account for it instead in the analysis of the research findings.

We now present additional examples illustrating why it is important to consider the various threats to validity and reliability in your project. An inappropriate account of these threats may, in the end, lead people to start questioning the overall quality of your work. For example, suppose that you have carried out interviews and have not allowed the interviewees to check your transcripts. You cannot then, in your analysis, make confident statements based on the material in the interviews, since you have not provided evidence to the reader that this is actually what the interviewee said in the interview. In this situation, an examiner may question your process of collecting and analysing data.

In another project, you may have used questionnaires to collect data. Suppose that you have developed the questionnaire on your own. When you started to collect the questionnaires, you realised that most people had misinterpreted your questions. An examiner may then question your entire work, since you will have collected data that does not match what you intended to collect, further implying that you are probably not able to conduct a useful analysis. In this example, the questionnaires should have been tested and revised before they were handed out.

In a computer science project, you intend to build a tool that measure the response time for database queries (e.g. SQL queries). You quickly develop the program and start to collect response times for various types of database queries. In this example, an examiner can question your entire project if it turns out that your program only measures a part of the whole query execution. In addition, your program might be sensitive to ad hoc values. For example, every time a database query contains the word "salary" the program crashes. An examiner may then argue that your program is not reliable enough.

If you choose to do a literature analysis, the use of a systematic approach is important to ensure the relevance of the collected material. Without a systematic approach, the resulting report from your work might be weak in terms of validity. There are a variety of reasons for this. Firstly, if you do not search the literature systematically, you cannot know if there are additional important sources which should have been considered. Secondly, without a comprehensive description of the chosen strategy for the literature analysis, it is very difficult for other people to assess the findings. Thirdly, as new material is continuously being published, there is a problem in knowing which sources have already been considered. Therefore, if the study has a long time-span, you run the risk of either omitting recently published material, or having to redo an extensive amount of the literature analysis.

In summary, in order to ensure that the reader can trust that relevant material has been included in your literature analysis, it is important that you think through and plan the *process* by which you address the question of relevance in your literature analysis. Similarly, it is important that you try to keep to your intended strategy. Should deviations occur, however, it is important that you acknowledge them and give motivations for them. In this situation, expert opinions such as those of your supervisor can be of great help in ensuring that important work has not been left out.

8.3   Methods

In the literature, there is little consensus about what counts as a method and what is understood to be a technique of data collection. By *technique* we mean various ways of undertaking data collection, interpreting data, and analysing collected data. However, in this book, we do not intend to address this issue of what separates techniques from methods. We will here take a rather pragmatic approach and present a set of methods and techniques which, in our view, are appropriate means of addressing the problem at hand.

8.3.1   Literature Analysis

By *literature analysis* we mean a systematic examination of a problem, by means of an analysis of published sources, undertaken with a specific purpose in mind. Hence, our use of the term 'literature analysis' here should not be confused with a review of existing work in an area, which you undertake in order to familiarise yourself what has already been done in your area.

In many projects there will be some need for a literature analysis. For example, if you have developed a program for analysing genome data, then you will need to contrast your program with similar programs that have been reported in the literature. If you have, instead, performed a comprehensive literature analysis on work done for benchmarking database transactions, most of your work will be centred on analysing the existing literature (e.g. making categorisations and detecting patterns). Hence, we dedicate a special section to validity and reliability issues that concern literature analysis, since it is relevant to most projects.

As already mentioned, in undertaking a literature analysis, it is important that you are aware of the potential consequences of the strategy you choose for searching and collecting material. Moreover, a careful interpretation and systematic analysis of each individual source is very important.

With the problem and specific objective established, i.e. what should be analysed, the next problem concerns appropriate use of *relevant* sources. In other words, how can you, in a literature analysis, ensure that you are considering the "right" sources, and "enough" of them?

There are a number of different techniques for identifying which sources are relevant to include in your literature analysis. You may use a combination of the following, in order to ensure that you have considered all *relevant* sources:

- Bibliographic databases – by searching or browsing their content using a sensible strategy, e.g. by using a set of keywords which your background reading and problem statement have identified as potentially relevant, by using a reference to a given source and locating additional sources
- Journals and conference proceedings – e.g. by browsing the table of contents in conference proceedings, or by searching for relevant articles using the search function at a journal's web site (most scientific journals are published simultaneously in printed and electronic format, and libraries that subscribe to the journal also usually have free access to the electronic version)

A related difficulty is that of *completeness*. One of the difficulties in a literature analysis is to know when one has collected enough material. In other words, at what stage should you stop collecting material? Of course, it is impossible to really know whether enough material has been considered, but the issue is of fundamental importance in terms of validity, i.e. whether the reader can trust your results. If you are aware of the process and the strategy for selecting sufficient material, then the likelihood is that the reader will also understand and appreciate your strategies, and will trust that enough material has been covered. This depends on your study, of course (its aim and objectives). The need for complete coverage of a specific aspect or angle of a phenomenon will vary. However, by undertaking a systematic process, which can be conveyed to the reader, the validity of the resulting study will be enhanced. The reader can understand why specific sources have been considered (and why particular sources have been left out).

Finally, expert opinions, such as your supervisor's, can be of great help in ensuring that your intended strategy is feasible. Also, as the process itself can be rather tiring and you may be faced with a mountain of material, an outsider's recommendations can help you decide whether to continue or not. It may be that at certain points in the process, depending on what emerges, you need to reconsider your strategy and try other techniques for ensuring relevance and completeness. In these situations, it is good to have someone monitoring your progress; someone who will be able to help by suggesting planned or unplanned deviations. If you do deviate from your plan, you should be able to give good reasons for doing so.

In literature analysis it is important that you acknowledge your own initial understandings of the phenomena being analysed. It is important that you minimise potential threats to validity by analysing, in a self-reflective way, your own behaviour during the research process.

For the results of your study to be trustworthy, it is important that you address both the process and outcome of the analysis properly. With respect to the process, you should emphasise both your strategy (i.e. what you planned), and the process of data collection and analysis (i.e. how you actually undertook your study). In addressing the issue of validity of the findings of your study, this is of key importance. Similarly, it is important that you acknowledge the sources on which your analysis is based. You should consider carefully why, and to what extent your sources are appropriate and relevant as a basis for your study.

8.3.2 Interview

Interviews can be undertaken in a variety of different ways, and to different ends. There are a number of different aspects which need to be considered when deciding on an appropriate form of interview for your study. Different styles of interviews have different strengths and weaknesses, and these are closely linked with your own ability, as a researcher, to undertake interviews. If you decide to use them, there are a number of issues to consider, both in terms of preparation and with respect to how they are carried out.

An *open interview* is a form of interview commonly used in qualitative research, where the researcher has no (or only limited) control of the issues raised during the interview session. So, even though the purpose of the interview is clear to the researcher, the specific issues to be covered during the interview session are not planned in advance. Instead, depending on what the interviewee emphasises during the session, the researcher tries to direct the session towards issues which he/she believes the interviewee finds especially important. When questions are asked, they should be phrased in such a way that they "open up" important issues. The interviewee should be allowed to use his/her own words during the session. In general, one should avoid leading and closed questions (i.e. questions to which there is a simple, perhaps even a "yes/no", answer). An open interview can be characterised as a form of interview in which "control" is very much in the hands of the interviewee. The advantage of using this style of interviewing is that, if it can be properly mastered, the issues which are of real importance to the interviewee will be addressed. On the negative side, open interview sessions can be difficult, especially for inexperienced interviewers. The difficulty lies in the need to achieve a suitable balance between genuinely open questions, and some more probing ones, which target important issues in a more focused way. After all, the outcome of a session should ultimately address the overall purpose for the interview. Furthermore, the open style can make it more difficult to take notes.

Related to these considerations is the need to address the issue of validity properly, and the especially relevant issue of researcher bias.

A closed interview is characterised by a fixed set of questions, which the interviewer asks during the session. This style of interview is sometimes also referred to as a pre-structured interview, as in its pure form, it does not allow adding or deleting questions depending on the replies. With respect to repeatability, it has an obvious advantage over the open interview. Its drawback, however, is that some questions might be regarded as being of limited relevance by the interviewee, which may influence his or her motivation to give a complete response. This style of interview is common in survey research, and is more suitable if you wish to use statistical methods to analyse the results.

Preparing and conducting interviews includes strategies for:

- *Selecting relevant interviewees.* For example, expert interviewees can provide very valuable data for your study, but it might be difficult to gain access to such people as they are likely to be very busy. Also to be considered are issues regarding who has the power to decide upon the allocation of the interviewees for the study, e.g. is it the organisation which decides that an interviewee will participate, or is participation in the study voluntary?

- *How to plan the structuring of the flow and interaction during the interview.* The extent of pre-structuring is a key issue here. For example, with open interviews there is limited control, whereas with closed interviews the interviewer has more control during the session. Note that a compromise may be found between these two pure forms.

- *The use of agendas during the interview.* Sometimes, the researcher has a number of issues which he/she wants to emphasise during the session, even though it is generally not critical that all are covered during the session.

- *How to collect and structure replies from interviewees.* For example, should the interviews use fixed answer alternatives and, if so, what alternatives, scales and measurements should be used (e.g. "1 = No improvements" and "5 = Major improvements")?

- *Whether or not to use an electronic device for recording interviews.* For example, with open interviews it might be difficult to take notes during sessions, and it may therefore be preferable to record them. Furthermore, if the interview is recorded, you can later accurately transcribe what was said. On the other hand, the use of any form of recording device may be regarded as a distraction and cause interviewees unease, leading perhaps to less valuable responses.

- *If preservation of confidentiality is necessary, and (in that case) how to preserve it.* This includes the appropriate handling of data that is collected in interviews; before, during and after the interview session. Preserving confidentiality relates to a number of issues, including: the notes themselves; the transcription of notes; notes made during analysis; and documents reporting the actual study. For example, should notes and tapes from interview sessions be destroyed after transcribing or after reporting the study, or should some form of agreement of non-exposure be established between involved parties? Here, it should be emphasised, that mistakes regarding these issues might be severely detrimental to the relationships between the parties involved in your study, and perhaps for forthcoming studies as well. Therefore, we strongly recommend that you discuss these issues with your supervisor.

- *Procedures for handling transcripts of field-notes, and how to allow interviewees to comment on and correct misinterpretations.* For example, if the interviewer transcribes field-notes from an interview session, what procedures should there be to allow interviewees to comment on, correct and make additions to the transcripts? Should there be any at all? This should be agreed on in advance of the interview sessions.

- *The logistics of conducting a session, e.g. where to conduct the interview.* If an interview is conducted in the interviewee's own workplace, he/she might feel more comfortable with the situation, but on the other hand it may be more difficult to arrange so that the session will not be disturbed.
- *To what extent there is a need to characterise the interviewees, and what aspects of their background that are of significance to the study.* This issue is closely related to the issue of anonymity in your study. In writing your report there are a number of potential pitfalls. For example, even though the name of a specific individual is not mentioned, it might be very easy for colleagues in the organisation to identify that person. Similarly, without providing the actual name of a company, if enough characteristics are provided, its identity might be indirectly revealed when it should not have been.

In summary, proper interviewing is heavily dependent upon trust, which needs to be established between the interviewee and the interviewer. Without it, the results from your study will be of limited value.

8.3.3   *Case Study*

A *case study* project is undertaken as an in-depth exploration of a phenomenon in its natural setting. A characteristic of a case study is that it involves a limited number of cases, sometimes even a single case. This allows you to undertake a detailed examination of the phenomenon. It has been suggested that the case study method is especially suitable when there is a desire to understand and explain a phenomenon in a field which is not yet well understood.

The actual *case* to be explored can be, for example, an organisation, a department (within an organisation), a group, an individual, or any other "unit", and the case study aims to understand and explain something within the unit. For example, a study may aim to explore how software developers use tools which support the software development process. The case study may then take place in a specific software development organisation, and focus on examining a certain kind of development tool. Thus, in this case study, the phenomenon to be explored would be a specific type of user and their use of the tool. Hence, the actual study might involve a group of developers who work in the organisation, and concern their perceptions of the role of a tool which they use in their work. However, in reporting from the study, you should aim to generalise from the specific details of the examined setting, attempting to characterise the situation for which the studied organisation is typical. It is important that enough detail is included for this to be possible.

In undertaking a case study, you will often be confronted with a large volume of data, which has complex inter-relationships. In addressing these, you will explore particular settings and cases in great detail. An aspect of case study projects, which needs careful consideration, is the extent to which the findings can, and should be, generalised. In reporting on a case study project, it is of fundamental importance that you can make a detailed characterisation of the important aspects of the case being explored. Otherwise, the value of the findings will be significantly decreased. The role and behaviour of the researcher in the study must also be considered, as a proper account is necessary for consideration of threats to validity (see Sect. 8.2). So, in planning for and designing a case study, it is important that you carefully elaborate on how a relevant choice of sites is to be made. Otherwise, if the chosen cases are not particularly representative of the focus for your study, the resulting findings will be of limited value.

During preparation and planning of a case study project, it is important that you carefully consider the availability of relevant cases. As with all methods that are to be applied in field-settings, there are a number of issues which you need to address in accounting for potential threats to validity in your findings.

8.3.4   Survey

Survey research is closely associated with the use of questionnaires, and statistical techniques for analysing their responses. Such research is often used for exploring a relatively well-known phenomenon, for which there exists a large sample of respondents having some knowledge of the issue of concern. For example, if you want to explore what the perceptions are in software development organisations concerning a specific, well-known methodology, you might investigate this by doing a survey. The advantage with this form of research is that, with relatively limited means, you can reach a large number of respondents, and thereby quickly cover a large number of informants. You can quickly reach a very large number of individuals and companies. Also, in a properly designed survey, you can control many uncertainties and estimate (using statistical techniques) the significance (see Chap. 10.2.3) of the findings. In addition, as questionnaires are often highly standardised, there is the possibility of automating the handling of responses.

An inherent characteristic of surveys is that it is difficult to investigate complicated issues. It is impossible to clarify questions, due to the lack of direct two-way communication between interviewer and interviewee. In fact, it is impossible to know that it is actually the targeted person that replies (or another company representative), and as you will be distanced from the data collection you have little control of this. Another drawback of surveys is that the motivation for participation is often low, and in general it is difficult to achieve high response rates. It has been said about survey research that it is impossible to know the true impressions of the respondents.

The techniques for how to properly set up a survey and statistically analyse its outcome are beyond the scope of this book. However, we recommend you to consider a few studies of reported survey research, as well as general texts on how to plan and carry out surveys.

8.3.5 *Implementation*

Many projects in computer science and information systems consist of developing
new solutions. Such a solution can consist of a new software architecture, method,
procedure, algorithm, or some other technique, which solves some problem in a
new way, which has some advantage over existing solutions. In a project of this
type, it is often necessary to implement the proposed solution, in order to demonstrate that it really does possess the proposed advantages. The goal of the implementation, then, is to demonstrate that the solution has certain properties, or that
(under certain conditions) it behaves in a specific way. This implementation often
needs to be compared with implementations of existing solutions, before conclusions can be drawn. The implementations of the existing solutions may or may not
be done by yourself.

When using the development of an implementation as your research method, it
is of course of vital importance to use good software development practice to
ensure the validity and reliability of your work. In this context, validity means that
your implementation properly reflects the solution that you propose. For an example, let us say that your proposed solution is an algorithm which includes the use of
a list of tasks being kept sorted in the order that they arrive, with new tasks being
added at the end of the list (i.e. a queue). If you incorrectly implement the algorithm
by having new tasks being added at the beginning of the list (i.e. a stack) your
implementation will not be a valid test of the solution that you proposed. The
implementation, which is your "instrument" for measuring the worth of the proposed algorithm, is actually measuring the worth of a different algorithm than the
one you have proposed, and your results will therefore lack validity.

Reliability, in this context, concerns the robustness of the implementation. In the
above example, you may have implemented the task list correctly (i.e. you have implemented it as a queue), but the implementation is otherwise faulty. If you were hoping
to show that the queue data structure gives certain performance advantages, you will
be unable to do so if the implementation is full of "bugs" and crashes too frequently.
In other words, you must make sure both that your implementation actually is an
implementation of the solution you propose (validity) and that the implementation
works well enough to be useful in your research (reliability).

Issues concerning validity and reliability also arise when deciding how to evaluate
the implementation. If you are proposing a new form of database architecture, and
make an implementation of this architecture, how should you use the implementation
to evaluate the advantages and disadvantages of the architecture? Similarly, if you are
proposing a new data mining algorithm for discovering patterns in data collected from
breast cancer patients, how should you best evaluate the usefulness of your
algorithm? How these questions are solved will depend largely on what type of solution you are proposing, and what the proposed advantages are. For example, a new
form of graphical user interface may be evaluated using human subjects who test
the interface and are subsequently interviewed. A new data mining algorithm, on the
other hand, may be evaluated by using a set of training data to set the parameters of

the algorithm, followed by using a set of test data to measure the accuracy of the predictions made by the algorithm. Although these implementation studies are very different from each other, you must in both cases make sure that your evaluation method leads to results which are both valid and reliable.

8.3.6 Experiment

An experiment focuses on investigating a few variables and the ways in which these are affected by the experimental conditions. Typically, experiments are used to verify or falsify a previously formulated hypothesis. For the purpose of experimental testing, the hypothesis is usually formulated as a causal relationship. An example of such a causal relationship is the hypothesis that including support for graphics in a particular type of software degrades its performance. Experiments are then designed and performed in such a way that the results will either support or falsify the hypothesis that graphics degrade the performance. It is important to note that a positive outcome in an experiment can never be said to "prove" that the hypothesis is correct. This is because there could always be some other explanation for the result. There is also an unlimited number of things that may go wrong in any experiment, and which may lead to erroneous and misleading results. Hence, we may say that a positive outcome lends some support to the hypothesis, ut we can never claim that it "proves" its correctness.

In the computer and information sciences experiments are often done by implementing a model of some system and running simulations to see how the model is affected by different variables. This again raises the issues discussed in Chap. 8.3.5 about validity and reliability of implementations, since the implementation must obviously correctly reflect the model. In addition, the model itself must also be a correct characterisation of the system being studied, which adds an additional level of difficulty to simulation as a research method.

If you are using experiments in your projects, you are advised to consult the literature on experimental design. When, for example, designing experiments involving human subjects you need to design the choice of subjects so as to ensure statistically valid results. There are many complex issues regarding experiment design that are beyond the scope of this book. Consulting additional literature and discussing the experimental design with your supervisor, should both be considered mandatory if you are planning to use this type of method.

8.3.7 Summary

Depending on which methods are relevant to your project, we recommend that you look for complementary sources and examples of previous work which have used the chosen methods. There is a rich body of literature focusing on methods, for example, Yin (1994), Denzin and Lincoln (1994), and Tichy (1998). Also, your supervisor is likely to have recommendations on relevant literature from your own specific area. It can be very illuminating to read other work from a method perspective, and it can provide valuable guidelines and hints on how to apply a specific method. For examples, see Jain (1991), Walsham and Waema (1994), Sampaio and Paton (1997), or Maansaari and Iivari (1999).

8.4   An Illustrative Analogy

To emphasise the characteristics of different methods, we will use an analogy from the field of sport. We hope that it helps to clarify some aspects concerning methods and their potential use in different problem situations.

Our discussion in this analogy is based on a number of different scenarios. We acknowledge that one may question the realism of some aspects in these scenarios. However, we hope that they can act as useful illustrations. For example, it would of course be very difficult to motivate the players of the team to play the number of matches necessary in order to fulfil the demands of a properly designed experiment (e.g. for achieving statistical significance).

Background – Context and actors in domain. Suppose that there is a soccer team playing in a soccer league (i.e. an organised competition), so that they will compete with a number of other teams in the league on a yearly basis. In this analogy, we will refer to the specific soccer team as "Hopeless United". The team consists of a set of players, and a coach. Among other duties, the coach decides on the strategy and tactics by which the team should play, and is responsible for the overall performance of the team (and consequently, also for each individual player's performance). The owners of the team have financial responsibility and are keen to receive some return on their invested money. Finally, the local newspaper writes a number of articles on Hopeless United.

Background to a study on the team. Last year, the team performed badly, and the different actors have a number of different approaches to how to tackle the problem of identifying factors that can improve the team's performance.

Thus, in this analogy we could say that there is a common aim for all the actors involved, namely: *to identify factors that can improve the team's performance.* Let us now consider how each actor tries to achieve this aim.

Scenario 1 – Owners. The owners are interested in what can be done in order for the team – as a whole – to improve their overall performance. This is based on an assumption that if the team plays well, there will be more spectators interested in watching the team's matches, with a consequential increase in funding from the sponsors of the team. Thereby, the individual performance of individual players would (in general) not be of specific interest. One obvious exception would probably be that of superstars, since if the team has such players, they would most likely be very popular amongst the spectators and fans. At a meeting two potential approaches emerge.

One approach would be to buy two promising new players; a goalkeeper and a forward. The owners hope that these two new players will make the team perform better; that the new forward will score more goals, and the new goalkeeper will make more saves. The owners of the team could evaluate the team's performance after a year, and then decide whether the new players should stay in the team or not. We could characterise this approach as a form of experiment during which the new players are tested.

Another approach would be to listen to other experts in the area for advice on what to do. We could characterise this approach as a *case study*, since probably only a few experts will be contacted. Thereby, the current situation in the team would be examined and analysed in the light of existing "theories" which a few other external experts have (i.e. each expert has his/her own view of how soccer should be played). Preferably, an open *interview* style would be used in order to capture the essence of what other experts think should be done to improve the team's performance.

Scenario 2 – Coach. The coach has tried, for a number of weeks, to figure out what to do about the current situation. Three potential approaches for dealing with the situation have emerged.

One is to gain an overview of what other people think is wrong and how the team can be improved. The reason for this is that the coach thinks that he is too close to the environment (i.e. managing the team, choosing strategy) and therefore needs some input from people who have a little more distance from his work. The coach decides that it would be useful to get some input from both current and former players, and members of the local supporters' club. We could characterise this approach as a form of *survey*, since the coach is seeking input from many people. As many people are involved, the input would probably need to be collected by using *questionnaires*. In addition, these questionnaires would need to be anonymous, in order for the players involved to feel confident that they can express their opinions freely.

Alternatively, the coach could ask some researchers at the nearby university for help. He has heard that the researchers have developed a computer program for testing different co-operation strategies amongst software agents. Furthermore, the researchers seem to have used a computer game for soccer simulation as their test environment. Hence, the coach hopes that the researchers can build a computer application that can explain various aspects of the strategy used by Hopeless United. In addition, the coach hopes that he can use this computer program to verify the hypothesis that the players score more goals when playing according to a particular tactic. We could characterise this approach as a form of *implementation*, since a computer program needs to be developed. The coach could then use the implementation to demonstrate specific aspects of the strategy that need to be improved. We could also characterise this approach as a form of *experiment*, since the coach plans to test some of his hypotheses, by adjusting the tactic used by the players, in order to verify (or falsify) that more goals are scored.

Finally, the coach could alter the team's current formation (two forwards, four midfields and four defenders) to a new formation (e.g. three forwards, four midfields and three defenders). The coach could then let the team play with the new formation for ten matches, and investigate whether there is any improvement in performance. We could characterise this approach as a form of *experiment*, since the coach plans to test a new formation over ten matches, and then investigate whether the new formation has improved the team's performance.

Scenario 3 – Local newspaper. The local newspaper plans to run a series of articles on why the team wins so few matches and what can be done in order to improve their performance. For these articles, they intend to go through their archive of articles and books on Hopeless United. The purpose is to provide a historical overview of how the team has evolved over the years, and investigate whether suggestions for improvement can be identified based on this historical overview. We could characterise this approach as a form of *literature analysis*, since many literature sources (books and newspaper articles) will be analysed.

Concluding remarks. As can be seen in these scenarios, they all share the same aim: *identify factors that can improve the team's performance.* Depending upon the viewpoint from which we consider the situation, we find that a wide range of methods can be used to reach the aim. Even when we consider a single actor and a single situation, it is evident that more than one method can be applied to reach the aim. Also, it is not obvious that a single method alone will be ideal. Instead, it is often the case that a combination of methods might lead to the best result.

8.5   A Four-Step Process

We here describe in overview four steps to be carried out in the process of identifying and describing the objectives of your project, and for choosing suitable methods to use to fulfil the objectives.

8.5.1   Develop Objectives

Once you have established a clear aim for your project, you can start to think about how you are going to achieve that aim. Try to think in terms of sub-goals (objectives) that will lead you towards the aim. Thus, by fulfilling each of the objectives you should reach the aim. For some objectives, it can be useful to write down the underpinning argument, so that you know why you are tackling each objective.

The scope of objectives can vary from institution to institution. Some institutions may require every task you perform, for example writing the report, to be described as an objective; other institutions may require only that you describe the practical work in terms of objectives. Most thesis projects do not require more than three to four objectives.

Here follows an example of an aim and its set of objectives.

Aim: Compare the current theory on X with how companies support X in practice.

Objectives:

- *Select companies.* Identify ten companies that work with X in practice. These companies should have been working with X for at least 5 years.
- *Select comparison criteria.* Comparison criteria need to be identified in order to be able to compare the current theory of X with the current practice of X. If such comparison criteria are not already available, e.g. in the literature, they will need to be invented.
- Investigate how companies work on X with respect to the comparison criteria.
- Analyse the results obtained from the companies and compare with what is being said in the literature on X.

8.5.2 Identify Potential Methods

Once you have written down your objectivities, you can start to identify potential methods for each objective. Think in terms of: how can this objective be achieved or solved?

For example, reconsider the objective: *investigate how companies work on X with respect to the comparison criteria.* This objective can be achieved using a number of different methods, e.g. questionnaires or interviews, which in turn should be broken down into different types of interviews etc. Write down only those methods that are relevant for your objective (in the context of your aim). Thus, there is no point in listing irrelevant methods just to show a large number of alternatives.

Once you have identified a potential method, briefly describe how it could be used to meet your objective and what the implications might be for your final result. In our example, you could describe the type of material which might be collected by conducting an interview, and how that material might affect the quality of the final result of the project.

8.5.3 Choose Among the Potential Methods

When you have identified a set of possible methods for an objective, you need to choose the one (or the ones) that you are going to use. Of course, each choice should be properly justified. Each method has its own advantages and disadvantages, and you need to choose the method that you believe will, in the end, give the final result of highest quality. For example, choosing a method that gives data of poor quality will, in the end, lower the quality of the final result of your work.

Do not make choices with arguments such as "due to time constraints, method X will not be chosen as a method". An examiner or supervisor can then respond with an argument such as "you have identified and described a method that not even in theory can be applied within the allowed time span of the project". What you can do is to mention the method that culd not be used due to time constraints in your discussion about future work. Perphaps the method that you could not use in your project can be used in a follow-up project in the future.

8.5.4   Present Details of the Chosen Approach

When you have chosen the methods you intend to use, it can be useful to summarise your overall approach. This serves at least two important purposes. First, you will be able to get a bird's eye view of the methods you have chosen and see their relationships. Second, you will be able to present additional details of how you intend to use these methods in your project. Additionally, it will be easier for other people to grasp your approach if you have provided a summary of how you intend to structure your work.

9
Following the Objectives

Once your problem description has passed the quality control (see Fig. 4.1), you can embark on actually doing the project. All you have to do now, unless something unforeseen happens, is to follow your objectives. They will guide you towards achieving the aim.

During the course of the project, you are likely to come across interesting aspects that were not known when you wrote down the aim. Sometimes these can sidetrack you away from the main purpose of your project. It is therefore important to refer back to the aim, and decide whether this new track falls within the scope of the project, or whether it should not be pursued and instead possibly be suggested as future work. Perhaps the aim should be updated so that the new issue can be smoothly incorporated into the project. Always discuss these things with your supervisor before you start adjusting the aim. Your supervisor might not fully appreciate that you have changed the aim and the focus of the project without discussing the motivation for the change, any possible implications, etc, with him or her first. (the agreed upon aim is your common goal and contract)

The meetings with your supervisor and the examiner are important checkpoints to monitor the project's progress and to give you valuable feedback. Do not underestimate the importance of these meetings; they can help you to avoid future problems.

If you find yourself in a situation where you cannot meet your objectives, it is important that you discuss it with your supervisor immediately. Here we list some advice for both students and supervisors on what to do in these situations. Risk levels range from 1 to 3, where 1 is a low risk and 3 denotes high risk of rejection by the examiner.

- Additional work (risk level 1). Can additional work, i.e. further experiments, simulations, interviews, reading etc. (depending on the chosen method) produce additional results which will meet your objectives and enable you to draw clear conclusions from your project?

Risks: The additional work may take too long to perform. If you start on additional work that you do not have time to complete, then you are wasting time which could have been spent on writing about conclusions drawn from the results you already have.

M. Berndtsson et al. (eds.), *Thesis Projects: A Guide for Students in Computer Science and Information Systems*.

Tip: Plan the time very well, and do not start on additional work unless you are 100% sure that you will be able to complete it. Discuss the time plan with your supervisor and make sure to follow the advice given.

- Alternative aims (risk level 2). Has your work resulted in some very interesting findings that were not stated in the aims and objectives of your report? In this case, it may be possible to update the initial parts of your report, and change your aims and/or objectives so that they correspond to the findings you have made.

Risks: If this is not done skilfully and with caution, you can end up with a report where different parts are inconsistent. The examiner is more likely to give you an unfavourable grade if you present a report where aims and objectives do not correspond, where results do not correspond to the objectives, or where the sections on background and related work[4] do not correspond to the aims and objectives. In some cases, you may end up rewriting all or most of the report.

Tips: Read the whole draft of your report and check carefully that everything makes sense and that the updates are consistent. Discuss the changes with your supervisor and present drafts of the changed report as quickly as possible.

- Failure analysis (risk level 3). Was the failure to meet the objectives caused by some unexpected problem, which may be of general interest? If so, it may be possible to "save" the project by adding a detailed analysis of this unexpected problem, and report that as the main finding of your project. Beware, however, that this will only convince the examiner if the unexpected problem is as interesting as the original problem described in your project proposal. This rarely happens. Also, be aware that this will require a lot of re-writing of the report, since the aims and objectives will not correspond with the results.

Risks: It is unusual for a problem you meet during the project to be interesting enough to be worth reporting. There is, therefore, a high risk of rejection by the examiner. It is also easy to underestimate the amount of re-writing needed in initial parts of the report.

Tips: Do not use this option unless you are in a desperate situation. Discuss everything in detail with your supervisor, and if possible with the examiner.

If none of these options work, it is most likely that the examiner will not give you a pass grade for your project. In such cases, it is important to find out what will happen as a consequence. This tend to vary significantly, depending on what course you are taking, at what level you are in your studies, in which department you are studying, at which university, and in what subject and so forth. It may also depend on your previous performance in other subjects in your studies. Regardless of all this, it is of greatest importance that you discuss the situation with your supervisor, examiner, study advisor or other persons who can give you information and advice on how to proceed.

---

[4] See Chapter 14 details on chapters related to background and related work.

10
Presenting and Analysing your Data

As you follow the objectives you will start to gather data (e.g. data from simulations, data from interviews, or data from literature analyses). The collected data needs to be properly presented to the reader. In Sects. 10.1 and 10.2 we briefly describe techniques and guidelines for how to present both non-numerical and numerical data.

Once the data has been presented, it can be analysed. Briefly, to analyse the data means that you evaluate the data against the objectives of your project. Guidelines for how to analyse your data are described in Sect. 10.3.

The outcome of the analysis represents your results (or findings). Section 10.4 discusses the nature of a good result, and the evaluation of a hypothesis in light of the data obtained.

10.1 Presenting Non-Numerical Data

In this section, we present guidelines for presenting non-numerical data such as:

- Data from a literature analysis
- Data from interviews
- Data from questionnaires
- Data from implementations

10.1.1 Presenting Data from a Literature Analysis

When you present what you have found in your literature analysis, the most important thing to keep in mind is its purpose in your project. This purpose must always be at the forefront when you decide how to structure your presentation. For example, if you are using a literature analysis as your method for identifying differences between two software engineering methods (for simplicity, we just call them

M. Berndtsson et al. (eds.), *Thesis Projects: A Guide for Students in Computer Science and Information Systems.*
© Springer 2008

method X and method Y), you can structure the presentation of the literature analysis in a number of different ways. Here follows two examples:

1. You can begin with a detailed description of method X, including quotes and excerpts from the literature you used. You should report any inconsistencies in the literature, for example, if some authors claim that method X is not suitable for a given type of system, whereas other authors claim the opposite. You should report the arguments that were used by each author to support his or her claims. The description of method X can be followed by a detailed description of method Y, using the same technique. You can then report what is said in other literature that has compared the two methods, if such literature exists.

2. You can begin by reporting what is said in the literature about desirable properties of software engineering methods. Again, you should report any differences or contradictions in the views of different authors, and state the arguments they are using to support their views. After this you can give detailed descriptions of the methods X and Y, which are to be compared in your study. The final part of your literature study can be to compare methods X and Y on the basis of the properties identified earlier. You should then report which of these properties are present in each method, and to what degree.

From the example above it should be clear that presenting the data of a literature analysis cannot be done simply by listing a set of quotes. Rather, it requires structuring the material in a way which is suitable for the purpose of the analysis. It also means carefully separating out the literature which is more useful for the analysis, from that which is less useful. You should generally not include a discussion of, or excerpt from, a source that you have read, if it turns out that it is not related to your project and will not have any impact on your work or aim. The amount of time you have spent reading a particular source is not relevant to whether it should be discussed in your analysis. Again, if you always keep in mind the purpose of the literature analysis in your project, this should not be a problem.

Quite often a literature analysis can be structured in such a way that it provides an argument for a certain idea or interpretation. This argument is then supported and exemplified with material from the literature. However, you should also include all important counter-arguments that you have found. For example, suppose your project is aimed at investigating the potential usefulness of neural networks for predicting crop harvests, and you have chosen literature analysis and implementation of a prototype system as your methods. Your literature analysis can then be structured as an argument for the usefulness of neural networks for this prediction task. As well as agricultural literature, it can also use literature about neural networks in general, and other literature, to support your arguments. Here are two possible examples of how to structure the literature analysis for this example project:

1. Start by describing in detail what properties neural networks have, using technical literature on this subject. Continue by describing previous work on crop harvest prediction, including work that has clearly identified and described the reasons

for shortcomings of earlier methods. This way, you can identify the properties that a method is expected to have in order to predict crop harvests successfully. You can then conclude your literature analysis by showing that the properties of neural networks match those identified in the literature as being successful. Finally, include any material you have found indicating that neural networks may fail in this task, and describe the arguments stated by those authors.

2. Start by describing in detail previous work in crop harvest prediction, including the literature that identifies the shortcomings of earlier methods. Describe in detail the properties of neural networks, as well as previous work on applying neural networks in different tasks. Show the similarity of some of these applications with the harvest prediction problem, by reviewing in more detail those parts of the literature that describe properties of the application problems. Use citations and excerpts of sections that you believe will convince the reader that a method that succeeds in a particular application should also succeed in crop harvest prediction. Finally, include any material you have found indicating that neural networks may fail in harvest prediction.

As the examples above illustrate, there are many different ways a literature analysis can be structured, and there is no "fixed" format to follow. You will have to develop the structure that is best suited for your particular project, the data you have found and the arguments you want to make in your analysis.

One of the best ways of learning how to present a literature analysis is to look at examples. You should study the examples of literature analysis you find in the literature you read during the project. In addition, you should make use of advice from your supervisor, since he or she is experienced in both writing and reading literature analyses. You can, for example, pick some examples you thought were good, and bring them to one of the meetings with your supervisor. Ask him or her to verify whether those analyses are good examples from which to learn. If your supervisor agrees to it, then it can be very useful to discuss one of the analyses in more detail later on. Identifying and analysing what was good and bad about another person's literature analysis can be a very useful way of learning how to write this part of the report.

10.1.2 Presenting Data from Interviews and Questionnaires

If you have conducted interviews, you will probably have a pile of tapes or notes that together represent your material from the interviews. This material must now be structured and presented to the reader in an appropriate form. In essence, you have to make a choice as to what to include, ranging from "exact" transcripts (word by word) of entire interviews, to summaries of each interview. You should discuss this choice with your supervisor.

If you have used questionnaires you probably want to present your data by using figures or tables (see Sect. 10.2).

Table 10.1 Different ways of structuring the presentation of collected data

	No grouping	Grouping	Summary
Structure by company	Company A • Q1 • Q2 • Qn Company B • Q1 • Q2 • Qn	Company A • Q1-Q5 • Q6-Q8 Company B • Q1-Q5	Company A • Summary of Q1-Qn Company B • Summary of Q1-Qn
Structure by question	Q1 • Company A • Company B Q2 • Company A • Company B Qn • Company A • Company B	Q1-Q5 • Company A • Company B Q9-Qn • Company A • Company B	Q1-Q5 • Summary of company A and B Q9-Qn • Summary of company A and B

What data from interviews and questionnaires might have in common is how you structure the presentation of the collected data. In Table 10.1, we present a number of different ways of structuring data from interviews and questionnaires. Your chosen method might restrict the number of alternatives you have for how to structure the data. For example, if you have performed an open interview it might be problematic (or even inappropriate) to arrange the material in sequential order (i.e. question 1 followed by question 2 etc.). So the enumerated alternatives in Table 10.1 should only be seen as a set of examples of how you can structure the data.

10.1.3   Presenting Data from Implementations

An implementation can be part of your method for various reasons, for example, if you rely on simulation data and need to implement the simulation model or the simulation tool yourself. In other cases you may implement a system in order to demonstrate that something can be done, or as part of testing a method for systems development. In all these cases, it is necessary to use good software development practice, part of which is to document the implementation well.

Since the implementation is part of your method for the project, you also have to show as much of the documentation as is needed in order to convince the reader that the implementation is correct. For example, you might have implemented an algorithm and performed some simulations where you compared it to another algorithm. Maybe you have already described the algorithm very clearly in your report, but in order to convince the reader that your simulation data are meaningful, you must also demonstrate that the simulations were done with a correct implementation of the algorithm. In other words, you must convince the reader that the differences observed between the algorithms are not caused by errors in the code.

So, how do you present the implementation in a way which convinces the reader that it is correct? One thing to rule out immediately is to simply list the code, and expect the reader to verify that it is correct. Computer implementations often contain thousands of lines of code, and even a short implementation of a hundred lines or so is hopelessly difficult to verify by manual inspection.

Instead, you have to demonstrate to the reader that you have used good software development practice, and show the steps in the process of developing the implementation. An example is to first show the algorithm in pseudo-code and explain relevant parts of the pseudo-code in writing. You can then show a graphical representation of the code, using, for example, flowcharts or some other graph format, which is appropriate for the particular algorithm at hand. This graphical representation should also be discussed in the text so that the reader has a very clear understanding of it (and is convinced that you do too). Finally, you can present relevant parts of the code, i.e. those parts that contain the key features of the implementation. This technique is particularly useful if you are using the implementation for the purpose of, for example, showing that a programming language or a model lacks (or contains) certain features. In that case, these code examples may be the main part of your data.

Figure 10.1 and 10.2 show brief examples of the description techniques outlined in the paragraph above. For further details about writing pseudo-code and using graphical representations of code you should consult introductory textbooks in computer science or software engineering. It is important to realise, however, that these techniques are not sufficient for all types of implementations in all types of projects. You may implement a much larger software where it is necessary to use higher-level description techniques, or you may implement safety-critical software where it is necessary to demonstrate that you have used a formal verification procedure to check the programs for correctness. In short, you should use the type of description technique which suits your project and type of implementation best, and apply it in such a way that you demonstrate to the reader that you have done a good job.

Additional tips:

- *Where to put code*. Most of the code you write should be placed as an appendix to the report. No one is going to read large amounts of code, and it is therefore just distracting to see it in the middle of the text. However, as mentioned earlier, you can include short sections of code within the text to demonstrate how particular implementation problems were solved, or to demonstrate the absence or presence of particular features. Code sections that are included in the text should be only a few lines long. If you are allowed to use supplementary media for your report, you can for example provide a CD-ROM containing the code, or make it available on a web site.

```
initialize( Hᵉ)
initialize( Hˢ)
initialize( Pᵉ)
initialize( Pˢ⁾
while (t < maxgen) do
    until ((h ∈ Hᵉ) and (h solves Pᵉ ∪ (Pˢ)))
    evaluate( Hᵉ, Pᵉ ∪ Pˢ
    reproduce( Hᵉ)
    t = t + 1
    end
    add h to Hˢ
    until ((p ∈ Pᵉ and (p defeats Hᵉ ∪ Hˢ))
    evaluate( Pᵉ, Hᵉ ∪ Hˢ)
    reproduce( Pᵉ)
    t = t + 1
    end
    add p to Pˢ
end
```

Fig. 10.1 Pseudo code representation of an example algorithm

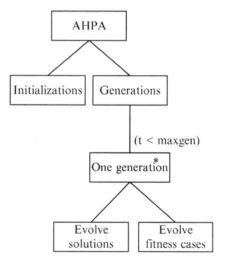

Fig. 10.2 Graph representation of the example algorithm from Fig. 10.1, using the Jackson Structured Programming graph conventions

- *Commenting.* All the rules of commenting code that apply in software engineering also apply to code written as part of a project. In other words, all code should be commented carefully and systematically. Any good textbook on software engineering will contain thorough guidelines on commenting. You should read those guidelines, and apply them meticulously.

- *Other information.* Depending on the purpose of the implementation, you may have to provide the reader with other information about the software. Examples include hardware and software requirements, user instructions etc.

If you have built a simulator you can also validate the implementation by using reference algorithms (i.e. baselines). By doing so you show that your implementation behaves correctly with respect to already established algorithms and baselines.

10.2 Presenting Numerical Data

In this section, we present guidelines for presenting numerical data, including:

- Using tables and graphs
- Avoiding misleading graphs
- Significance tests

10.2.1 Using Tables and Graphs

Consider the example data in Table 10.2. It is relatively clear how the update time depends on the number of tuples. We can see just from reading through the numbers in the right-hand column that update time approximately doubles for each row, i.e. for each increment of 10,000 tuples. However, this dependence is even more clear if we plot the update time against the number of tuples, as has been done in Fig. 10.3. This type of graph is called a line plot, and this simple form of graph is sufficient for the data we have in this example. The graph gives an immediate impression of

Table. 10.2 Example table showing how update time depends on the number of database tuples for two algorithms that are being compared in an example project. Each update time is the average from ten simulations

| Tuples (× 1,000) | Update time (seconds) | |
	Old algorithm	New algorithm
10	0.8	1.1
20	1.6	2.1
30	2.5	3.2
40	3.3	3.9
50	6.2	5.1
60	8.9	7.5
70	19.6	9.9
80	36.4	11.3
90	59.7	15.4
100	108.2	20.3

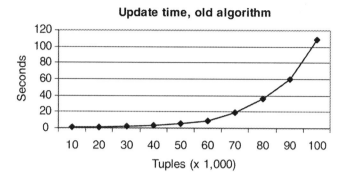

Fig. 10.3 Line plot showing performance, i.e. update time of the old database access algorithm. All update times plotted are averages of ten simulations

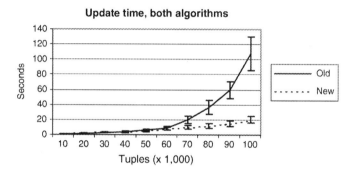

Fig. 10.4 Line plot showing performance comparison between two database access algorithms

the dependence of update time on the number of tuples, indicating that update time increases exponentially with the number of tuples. It is customary to organise line plots in such a way that the values of the independent variable appear on the *x*-axis, and those of the dependent variable on the *y*-axis.

In Fig. 10.4, we have added a second dependent variable to the line plot. This one shows the update time for the proposed new algorithm. It is immediately visible to the reader that the new algorithm appears to scale better to situations with large numbers of tuples. Another detail that has been added in the new graph is a set of error bars, showing the variation in average update time for each numer of tuples.

The two algorithms appear to perform approximately equally in the range 10,000–60,000 tuples, so therefore it is not apparent from the graph whether we can draw the conclusion that the new algorithm is better overall for the investigated interval. It is therefore necessary to show the lower part of the interval in more detail, and one way of doing this is simply to plot the range 10,000–60,000 tuples in a separate graph (another alternative could be to use a log-scale for the *y*-axis).

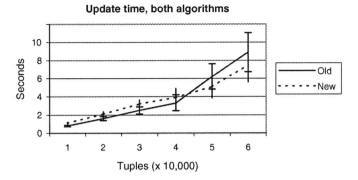

Fig. 10.5 Line plot showing performance comparison between two database access algorithms. Same as the graph in Fig. 10.4, except that only the interval 10,000–60,000 tuples is included

This is done in Fig. 10.5, and it indeed shows that the new algorithm performs worse than the standard algorithm for the interval 10,000–40,000 tuples. On the other hand, the difference between the two algorithms is very small in this interval, resulting in an overlap between the error bars. This means that the small difference can probably be explained as chance variation, rather than being a real difference in performance between the algorithms.

10.2.2 Avoiding Misleading Graphs

When choosing which interval to plot in the line graph, it is important to keep in mind that you can easily give a false impression by showing too narrow an interval. Consider choosing to plot the interval 10,000–40,000 tuples in Fig. 10.5. If it is not clearly pointed out to the reader that such a plot is a complement to the one for the whole interval, in Fig. 10.4, the graph may give the misleading impression that the new algorithm is worse than the old one. This misleading impression could of course also arise from the table, if we were to include only rows 1–4 in Table 10.2.

The purpose of using graphs is to make numerical data easier to understand by visualising them. We saw an example of this in Sect. 10.2.1 where line plots were used to visualise the data from Table 10.2. However, since these visualisations can be done in different ways, it is also possible to give the reader different impressions of the data. To some extent, this is good, since different interpretations are possible, but there is also the risk of giving false or misleading impressions.

An example of a misleading graph is shown in Fig. 10.6. It contains a column plot where the y-axis has been cut so that it starts at 0.75, rather than at zero. The consequence of this is that the differences between the algorithms seem bigger than they really are. This should be obvious by considering the difference at 10,000 tuples, where the column for the new algorithm is about ten times higher than that

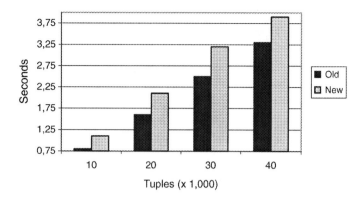

Fig. 10.6 Misleading column plot, which makes the difference between the old and new algorithm seem larger by letting the *y*-axis begin at 0.75 s

for the old algorithm, although the real difference is that the new algorithm takes 1.1 s and the old 0.8 s. The new algorithm thus takes 37% longer to execute than the old one, which means that the column should only be 37% higher. This discrepancy decreases further up the *x*-axis, but is present throughout the whole graph. At 20,000 tuples, the column for the new algorithm is 55% higher than the column for the old algorithm, but Table 10.2. shows that the new algorithm took only 31% longer to execute than the old one (2.1 and 1.6 s, respectively).

There are tools available today for drawing graphs very rapidly by automating part of the process. Some of these tools are easy to learn, and very efficient to use for generating graphs for your report. A drawback, however, is that they can sometimes automatically create misleading graphs. The shortening of the *y*-axis of Fig. 10.6, for example, may be done automatically by some tools. You must therefore inspect the graph carefully, and correct any mistakes made by the tool.

10.2.3   Significance Tests

You may be presenting a numerical comparison of data from experiments or simulations where you have varied one parameter. In such a case, if the system you have studied is stochastic, i.e. if the outcome of an individual run depends to some degree on chance, then it will be necessary to repeat each parameter setting a number of times in order to present the average result from a number of runs. This is because a single run can produce an untypical result by chance. Thus, it is important that any results that are going to be considered when drawing conclusions, are not just random effects. This can be done by applying a test for statistical significance.

As an example, we can observe that the advantages of the old algorithm in Fig. 10.4 were not statistically significant, since the error bars overlap for every plotted point in the interval 10,000–60,000 tuples. The differences between the algorithms do, however, seem to be significant for all points above 60,000 tuples. In summary, this means that we can say that these experiments indicate that the new algorithm is advantageous for 70,000–100,000 tuples, but that neither an advantage nor disadvantage was found for smaller numbers of tuples.

It is of vital importance, before attempting to draw any conclusions from data obtained through experiments or simulations, that you apply a suitable test for statistical significance. Failure to do so means that you run the risk of drawing incorrect conclusions, and – of course – that your examiner rejects the conclusions you propose, since they have not been shown to be significant. Which significance test fits your data will depend on the experimental set up and the type of data you have generated, and this is too large an issue to discuss in detail in this book. You are therefore strongly advised to consult the statistics literature and to seek the advice of your supervisor on this important issue.

10.3 Analyse Your Data

By analysing data, we mean that the data is systematically evaluated against the objectives of your project. The most systematic way of doing this is to go through one objective at a time, and evaluate the collected data against the objective. If all objectives have been satisfied, you can conclude that the aim of the project has been achieved. The details of this process of analysing whether an objective has been satisfied or not, depend on the type of project, and will therefore be described in more detail for the separate cases.

10.3.1 Descriptive Projects

In a descriptive project, you will have carried out a survey where the objectives state what research questions the survey is meant to answer. Let us consider the aim and objectives of the first example project in Sect. 5.2.1. The aim of this project was to "categorise and compare previous work within a subject area". We assume that you have already collected, read and presented the relevant data (e.g. previous research articles).

According to the first objective, you should "categorise previous work". In order to fulfil this objective you need to analyse the collected data against the first objective. You need to justify how and why you have developed the different categories, and why you have placed a particular data item in a specific category. The result of this objective is your categorisation.

In the second objective, you should "select a comparison criterion" in order to compare the collected data later. In order to fulfil this objective you need to choose comparison criteria. Earlier in the project, you may have identified several different factors (e.g. security, performance, usability, functionality) that could be used as comparison criteria. You may even have come across already existing and well-used comparison criteria. If you have several potential comparison criteria, you need to justify why you include some of them in your set of criteria, and why you exclude the other ones. The result of this objective is your set of comparison criteria, which include different factors that will be evaluated against the collected data.

In the third objective, you should "compare the previous work with respect to the comparison criteria". In order to fulfil this objective you need to evaluate the comparison criteria against the collected (and categorised) data items. The result of this objective may be to ascertain to what degree your collected data (i.e. the previous work) support the different factors that are part of your comparison criteria. For example, you may find that the earlier work was weak in terms of security issues, whereas recent work is strong regarding security issues.

10.3.2   Theory Oriented Projects

In a project with a strong theoretical emphasis, you may have extended or compared existing theoretical models, without testing them in practice. Let us consider the aim and objectives of the first example project in Sect. 5.2.2. The aim of this project was to "extend an already existing theory or model". We assume that you have already collected, read and presented the relevant data (i.e. the existing theory or model).

According to the first objective, you should "identify the details of the extension". In order to fulfil this objective you need to analyse the collected data (e.g. details of possible extensions). In this example, you would identify which features should be included in the extension. You will then need to justify why some features are more relevant than others. The result of this objective is your detailed description of the extension.

In the second objective, you should "introduce the extension to the original theoretical model". In order to fulfil this objective you need to first introduce the extension to the original model. It further implies that you need to verify that the extension is correctly introduced. The result of this objective is a new theoretical model composed of the original theoretical model and the extension.

In the third objective, you should "compare the original theoretical model with the extended version". In order to fulfil this objective you need to compare the two models against some comparison criteria. The result of this objective may be to ascertain whether the new model has better support for some features than the old model.

10.3.3   Applied Projects

In an applied project, you may have conducted experiments and gained experience from them. Let us consider the aim and objectives of the example project in Sect. 5.2.3. The aim of this project was to "gain experience from applying a theoretical model".

In the first objective, you should "set up a simulator for caching of web data". In order to satisfy this objective you need to design and implement the simulator. It further implies that you need to justify that the simulator is valid and correct with respect to existing baselines. The result of this objective is a simulator that can be used in your further experiments.

In the second objective, you should "implement the new algorithm". In order to satisfy this objective you need to implement the algorithm by the aid of the simulator. You need to justify that you have implemented the algorithm correctly in the simulator. The result of this objective is an implementation of the new algorithm in the simulator.

In the third objective, you should "test and analyze the new algorithm". This includes setting up relevant test scenarios and analyze them. Investigate the outcome of each scenario. Can you, for each scenario, explain the result of the experiment? Furthermore, you should see if you can identify any patterns in the results of the experiments. It may be possible to make a categorisation of the results of the experiments. The result of this objective is your explanation and categorisation of the results obtained from the experiments.

In the forth objective, you should "identify refinements to the design of the algorithm". In order to satisfy this objective you need to investigate the result of the third objective. Based on what you found in the third objective, can you suggest any refinements to the design of the algorithm? The result of this objective is your recommendation for refinements to the design of the algorithm.

10.3.4 A Comparison of Theory and Practice

As mentioned earlier, projects that combine theory and practice usually contrast the theory with current practice in companies or organisations. Let us consider the aim and objectives of the example project in Sect. 5.2.4. The aim of this project was to "contrast the current theory relating to a particular subject with how companies and organisations support it in practice".

In the first objective, you should "select companies or organisations" to be investigated. You will also need to provide justifications for why certain companies or organisations are not part of your investigation. The result of this objective is your list of companies and organisations that should be investigated.

In the second objective, you should "select comparison criteria". In order to fulfil this objective you need to select features of a particular subject and justify your investigation of them. This is needed in order to be able to do a comparison in objective number five. The result of this objective is your set of comparison criteria.

In the third objective, you should "investigate the details of the theory of the particular subject". This implies that you evaluate the theory against the comparison criteria. The result of this objective is to ascertain to what degree the theory supports the comparison criteria.

In the fourth objective, you should "investigate how companies or organisations work with the particular subject in practice". In order to fulfil this objective you need to evaluate how the particular subject is supported in practice against the comparison criteria. The result of this objective is to ascertain to what degree the comparison criteria are supported in practice.

In the fifth objective, you should "compare the results obtained from the second and third objectives". In order to fulfil this objective you need to evaluate the results obtained from the third and fourth objective. Are there any similarities or differences? Can you explain the reasons for the similarities and differences? The result of this objective is your identification of similarities and differences between the theory and how companies and organisations support the subject in practice.

10.4   What is a Good Result?

A good result is one where a *clear conclusion* can be drawn with *strong confidence*. From the viewpoint of determining the success of the project, it does not matter whether the conclusion is that the hypothesis is supported or falsified. In the example project from Sect. 10.2, the data can be satisfying and the project successful, regardless of whether the experiments show that the new algorithm was better or worse than the old algorithm. As long as the data allows you to draw clear conclusions with strong confidence, your work has been performed with success.

So, what does it mean that you can draw clear conclusions from the data? First, it means that you have set up the experiments and applied the methods in such a way that you can trust the data. Secondly, it means that you have conducted your presentation and analysis of the data thoroughly, without introducing any errors. Having done these things, you are able to draw clear conclusions, which are reliable and trustworthy. In other words, you have done your work.

There is a potential fallacy here, because your conclusions may be influenced by a wish to see a particular outcome. In the example mentioned above, you may have spent a lot of time developing, implementing, and testing the new algorithm. You therefore hope to see that it is better than previous algorithms, so that you can present your algorithm as a better solution than anyone else's. In this situation, it is important to keep in mind that your subjective wish to see one algorithm "win" over another must not influence how you view the data. Your job is to make an objective assessment of the two algorithms, and present the data. As long as you apply sound methodology in performing the assessment, your project will be successful, regardless of which algorithm turns out to be the better one.

If your project is based on an explicitly stated hypothesis, then it is necessary to evaluate whether this hypothesis is falsified or supported by the data. The hypothesis should summarise the aim of the project, stating it in the form of a proposition which can be tested. The whole project should then be focused on the testing of this proposition, and evaluating whether the data support or falsify the proposition.

11
Drawing your Conclusions and Identifying Future Work

The most important thing to remember about the conclusion section of your report is that it must refer back to the aim and objectives. For example, if you have stated a specific hypothesis, the conclusion section of your report should discuss whether this hypothesis still holds after completion of your work. Was the hypothesis supported by your experiments or investigation, or does the outcome show that the hypothesis no longer holds? In the latter case, you might propose a new, revised hypothesis, which may then become the basis of future work in your area. Alternatively, you should at least give some feasible explanations for why the current hypothesis does not hold.

The conclusions should also put your results into a wider context. For example, suppose that you found that a particular type of modelling method for relational data could express some object-oriented features, what would this mean in a wider context? We could perhaps say that there is no need to develop new modelling methods. This possible conclusion should be discussed. You should present supporting arguments as well as all the counter-arguments you can think of. In addition, you should make an analysis of your project in terms of identifying its weak and its strong points. In other words, go back over all the steps in the process and make an assessment of what you did right, and what mistakes you made. One reason for this is that you help the reader to identify those weak and strong points. In addition, by doing such an evaluation of your own work, you are demonstrating your knowledge of how a project should be done. You may have made some mistakes along the way, but you now have an opportunity to show your awareness of those mistakes and of the impact they may have had on the outcome of the project.

Finally, you should also identify the most relevant future directions relating to your work. It is rarely the case that a project presents the definitive answer to a research question, or the optimal solution to a problem. Given this, it is part of your job to identify further work of two kinds: work you would do yourself if you were continuing with the same project; and work you would suggest for other projects. One reason for doing this is that it makes your report more interesting if you provide suggestions for people who may consider continuing your work. It also places your work in a wider context, and shows that you understand how it fits into the general progress in your field. Most importantly, you are the one in the best position

M. Berndtsson et al. (eds.), *Thesis Projects: A Guide for Students in Computer Science and Information Systems.*
© Springer 2008

to point out future directions, given your experiences from doing the project. In the following sections we discuss these issues in more detail.

11.1 Summarising the Results

Whereas the results chapter (see Chap. 14 for details) provides a thorough presentation and analysis of your results, the conclusions chapter should give a summary of the results. This is because the conclusions chapter is "built" around the results, and makes use of the results in various ways: putting them into context, evaluating them in the light of how the project was carried out, and identifying how they can be extended through future work. The summary of results makes the discussion easier to read without having to go back to the results chapter.

In order to write this summary, it is useful to think of certain questions, such as: "What were the main findings in the results chapter?" For example, you may have been able to show that there was a statistically significant difference between how quickly users became proficient in using software when they had access to online documentation, and when they only had a printed manual. In the results chapter, you may have used several pages to show the detailed results of your experiment, and to explain the statistical test that you applied to test for significance. In the conclusions chapter, however, this can be summarised in a few sentences.

Another useful question to ask yourself is: "What was I able to show with confidence, and what was uncertain?" The summary of results should differentiate between certain results and less certain ones, since these must be treated differently in the subsequent discussion and evaluation. For a very certain result, it is highly relevant to discuss what the impact of the result on the subject area may be, and in what ways the result will be useful in the future. For an uncertain result, however, it is more relevant to discuss what further work needs be done in order to obtain a more certain result.

11.2 Putting the Results into Context

After summarising the results, the next step is to discuss how they fit into the wider context of the subject area as a whole. By doing this, you help the reader understand the impact, meaning and usefulness of your work. In a sense, this is the most important section of your whole report, because it is here that the whole point of the work and its results is explained.

Just as with the summary of results, you can develop your writing of the conclusions by asking yourself a number of questions. We here outline some examples of typical questions that may help you.

"What can my results be used for?" This is perhaps the most interesting point for a reader of your report. Some readers may actually be uninterested in your

report until they read what the results can be used for, and only then will they start looking into what you did exactly, how you arrived at those results, or how your proposed solution to some problem works.

"Who can use my findings, and in what different ways?" For example, if your results show that staff using software for computer-supported co-operative work was more productive than staff that did not, then it is also part of your work to discuss who can use this result. In this example, perhaps the result will be most useful for large corporations, and much less relevant for smaller ones. Or maybe your investigation was limited to studying staff in a particular industry. In that case, you should remind the reader of this fact, and give your thoughts on whether the result is applicable to other industries or not.

"Have I made a contribution to my field of research?" This is a very important question, since the goal of research is to advance understanding of the subject. You should therefore identify any contribution you have made, and its level of importance. For an undergraduate project, the contribution may be relatively small, since the available time is limited, and because you are just beginning to learn the skills of research. However, it is still possible to make a real contribution in an undergraduate project, and it does happen that the findings from undergraduate projects make their way into research articles.

"Are there related research areas which may benefit from my results?" For example, if your project has resulted in a new algorithm for data mining in image data, it is entirely possible that the same algorithm could be very useful for data mining in other types of data. Perhaps the algorithm could also be used for applications other than data mining. In that case, you should also discuss briefly what adaptations of the algorithm would be necessary for the alternative application. Identifying potential spin-offs is necessary to make your work interesting to a wider audience. It is also one of the ways in which science progresses – methods developed in one field turn out to be useful in other fields, with some modifications, and then the modified version may be adopted in yet another field.

"Are my results useful in real-world applications, or are they a contribution of a theoretical nature, so that they deepen our understanding of the subject?" You should answer this question in your report, and give reasons for why you think the results are useful in each case. If the results are mainly theoretical, you should discuss how they could potentially lead to practical applications. Similarly, if the results are mainly practical, you should describe ways in which they could be developed into a theory, or lead to modifications or additions to an existing theory.

"How do my results compare with those of others?" Parts of this comparison have probably already been done in the analysis section, but in the conclusions, you can make additional comparisons with related work. Whereas the analysis section may have contained a detailed comparison with an alternative approach, the conclusions section can bring up additional related works and give less detailed comparisons with these.

"Are my findings in line with other related work?" You should give an assessment of whether your results confirm the existing framework in your field, or whether they constitute something fundamentally new which could overturn the

existing theories in the field. If your results contradict a lot of the important related work, then you must have an extended discussion of the possible causes of this. As a general rule, the more "controversial" your results are, the more you have to provide strong arguments to convince readers that your results and conclusions are correct.

11.3   Evaluating the Process

Another part of the conclusions chapter should be an evaluation of your work. The importance of this section is that it helps the reader see the weak and strong points of the work, which is useful in deciding which of your results can be trusted most. So after having discussed the usefulness of your findings, you must also discuss to what degree they can be trusted.

You can develop this evaluation by going back to each step of the process and identifying weaknesses and any mistakes that have become apparent. You could do this both by trying to remember mistakes, and by reading through the report and trying to spot mistakes as you read. For each mistake you identify, think about what consequences it may have had on subsequent steps of the process, and what this could mean for the results. To give a very small example, suppose that you have compared the accuracy of two expert systems in monitoring a production process and deciding when the process should be stopped. Perhaps you tested each system on five test scenarios, but later realised that there were another three relevant scenarios that should have been included. In this case, describe what aspects of the systems' performance that have not been tested. Perhaps it is also possible to suggest how the two systems would have been likely to perform on the three additional test scenarios, based on what you know about them?

In addition to looking for mistakes, you should of course also try to identify the good decisions you made during the process. If you produced an excellent experimental design which allows you with high confidence to ensure the correctness and validity of your results, you should point this out in the conclusions. In general, you should think about how each good decision you made contributed to the results.

11.4   Identifying Future Work

This is an important part of your report, since a good 'future work' section not only convinces the examiner that you know how your work fits into the overall development of the subject area, but also helps readers to plan new projects using your work as a starting point. In a longer perspective, it will actually be possible to evaluate the significance of your work by looking at the number and quality of projects that have used it as a starting point. As with some other sections, it is possible to develop this one by asking yourself a number of questions:

"Of the objectives I had, are there any that are still not fulfilled?" For each of these, think of what you would need to do in order to fulfil them. It is not acceptable to have a great many of your objectives left unfulfilled, but you may have one or two which were only partially completed. This represents the most obvious future work, so start by describing how you would go about it.

"If I had more time to devote to my project, what would be the most important things to do?" Note that this is different from the previous point. What is meant here is that you should think of the most important and possible continuations of your project, after the current objectives have been fulfilled. As an example, perhaps your project has identified the factors that are most important for improving the communication protocols for distributed database systems, which was also the aim of the project. A natural extension would then be to develop a new communication protocol that would have an improved capability on the factors identified in your project.

"Have my results revealed new open questions which need to be addressed?" Quite often, you reach a result that answers the problem you are addressing, and successfully answers the questions you started with, but which also leads to some new questions. As an example, you may have investigated computerised methods for analysing the data from a type of biomedical experiment that gives information on the activity levels of thousands of genes. Perhaps you discovered that a simple form of clustering algorithm performed very well on this task, but you also found that there is a problem in how to help users interpret the resulting clusters, since there is so much data in each clustering. You could then suggest future work to develop visualisation techniques that could help the biomedical laboratory staff to interpret the clusters produced by your algorithm.

If your results are theoretical, you can ask yourself: *"What still needs to be done before my results can be applied in practice?"* You should then go on to explain the steps in this process, and give estimates of how much work there is to be done in each step.

12
Presenting and Defending your Work Orally

This chapter helps you in preparing for presenting and defending your work orally, as well as acting as an opponent.

12.1 Oral Presentation

What characterises a good oral presentation? One of the main difficulties with planning a good oral presentation is how to find the right balance between (1) including enough detail to make the project understandable to the audience, and (2) not including so much detail that the presentation fails to fit within the time assigned for it. To succeed in striking the right balance, you must plan your presentation thoroughly. In particular, you should carefully select which details to be included in the presentation, and which to leave out. You should also think about how those details should be presented so that the audience can grasp them as quickly and clearly as possible.

A good oral presentation is characterised by being clear, to the point, interesting, and, of course, inspiring. All of these characteristics can be achieved only by planning the presentation well. Planning not only allows you to be clear and to the point, it also makes helps you to be at ease and comfortable during the presentation. Feeling confident in the quality of your presentation is the key to being able to convince and inspire the audience. However, it should be kept in mind that academic presentations are meant to communicate a message, rather than merely to entertain. In other words, you can usually get away with being boring, if what you say is well-organised and clear; but you cannot get away by being entertaining without a well-founded and well-communicated message.

In this book we assume that you will use slides for your oral presentation. You can either use a slide projector and transparencies or a computer connected to a video projector. Slides are convenient to use as they help you to communicate and emphasise your message to the audience.

M. Berndtsson et al. (eds.), *Thesis Projects: A Guide for Students in Computer Science and Information Systems.*
© Springer 2008

12.1.1   Before the Presentation

The first two key steps in planning a presentation are to decide what to say and in what order. Thereafter you can proceed with the details of how to say it. In other words, you should begin thinking about your key message(s) and developing a structure for your presentation, and then fill in the details. One of the advantages of developing the structure first, is that you will know beforehand approximately how many slides you will have time to present. The structure makes it much easier to keep track of how much space you can use for each part of the presentation. Another advantage of developing the structure first, is that it makes it much easier to discuss the presentation with your supervisor. By having the structure in mind, you are more clearly aware of what things you want to say and in what order, and can therefore more easily discuss what to leave out, how to reorder, or which parts to change. Keeping the structure in mind helps you see any consequences of a particular change more clearly.

An example presentation structure is shown in Fig. 12.1. It is assumed in the example that the time allowed is 20 min and that questions are asked after the presentation. The first two slides (title page and outline) are used to introduce the speaker and the talk. It is usually a good idea to present and define key concepts before the aim is presented. Hence, two slides have been allocated to the explanation and definition of important concepts (the "background" slide), and to the presentation of the arguments behind the aim. One slide has been allocated to the aim and objectives of the project. Two slides are allocated to a description of how you approached the problem, your method etc. Two slides are allocated to the presentation of the results. Note that this example structure does not allocate any slides to a presentation of the data collected, which may or may not be necessary, depending on the project. The presentation finishes with two slides of your conclusions and suggestions for future work. In general, it is here assumed that each slide will take 2 min to present and explain. This will of course vary, depending on the content of each slide. You should of course make trial presentations and check how long it actually takes you to give your talk.

Content	Slides
Title Page	1
Outline	1
Background	1
Arguments	1
Aim and objectives	1
Approach	2
Results	2
Conclusions	1
Future work	1
Total	11

Fig. 12.1 An example presentation structure

Once you have such a presentation structure, it is time to start filling in the details. This often leads to a rearrangement of the structure, but maintaining a structure document, and updating it for every change can be a good way of keeping to the goal of a fixed number of slides. Otherwise, it is easy to end up with so many slides that there is no way you can present all your material.

When filling in the details, there are some basic rules to follow in the preparation of each slide. These rules all have to do with the clarity of presentation. Keep in mind that a slide with too much detail may be informative for you, but is really useless for those in the audience who cannot see its small print or do not have time to read everything. In other words, keep each slide clear, concise and to the point.

Here is a set of guidelines for preparing slides:

- *Layout.* Try to use a consistent layout on all (or most) of your slides. This makes your presentation easier to understand, since the audience can focus on the content of each slide, rather than trying to figure out where different things are located. Using a consistent layout means, for instance, placing the heading at the same position, using bullets and font sizes in a consistent way, and striving to have a consistent strategy for where to place figures in relation to text.

- *Font size.* One of the worst mistakes is to use a font that is so small that the audience cannot read the slide. Again, if the information is not readable, then you might as well have no slides at all! Thus, keep in mind that the whole audience should be able to read the text, and not only those sitting in the front rows. Exactly what font size is needed will of course depend on the size of the room. So the best thing to do, is to go to the room where the presentation is to be held, and try out some slides with varying font sizes. It is also worthwhile to keep in mind that the default text size, used in some tools for making slides, is 32 point. You can of course adjust this, but generally speaking, the font should never be smaller than 18 points for the body of the text.

- *Portrait or landscape orientation.* Which orientation is most suitable will depend on the content of the slide. However, you should try to use a consistent orientation throughout your presentation. Landscape is normally the preferred orientation.

- *Language.* Use short expressions. Space on slides is limited. Instead of the sentence "The evaluation of the implemented method shows that it was 22% slower than the current standard method", write something like "Implemented method 22% slower than standard". Keep in mind that what is written on the slides is complemented by what you say when talking about it, so shortened phrases on the slides are explained during the talk. On the other hand, this is a matter of striking the right balance – the text on the slides should be short, but not too cryptic.

- *Emphasis.* Sometimes, having a lot of text on a slide is unavoidable, for example when showing quotes. If it is difficult to parse the text and grasp the meaning quickly, then you can help the audience by emphasising important words or concepts using boldface or underlining.
- *Figures.* To help the audience interpret what you are saying, make use of visualisation techniques instead of relying just on text. If you include a mathematical formula, you can often visualise the relationship between the variables with a graph. If you have implemented some software, you can use a drawing to show its main components and how they relate. If you describe the steps of a process, you can draw a diagram of those steps and how each step relies on input from previous ones. In other words, for almost any kind of message, it is possible to use some kind of visualisation technique to facilitate interpretation. On the other hand, remember that things must also be spelled out in words – a presentation that relies too much on figures, without proper explanation in words, can also become vague and difficult to grasp.
- *Number of words.* Handbooks on how to make presentations will give you different advice on approximately how many words you can have on each slide. This will vary with the size of the room, average length of the words, the orientation, and if you have any figures on the slide. A rule of thumb that we suggest is to strive to have a maximum of approximately seven rows of text and seven words per row. This "seven by seven" rule of thumb corresponds roughly with what most other authors suggest, and has the advantage of being easy to remember.
- *Numbering of slides.* Put a small slide number in the lower right hand corner of each slide. The number should be small and sufficiently close to the edge of the slide not be confused with the contents. Anyone asking questions after your presentation can then refer to the slide number in the question, and you can more easily find the slide referred to.
- *Use of headings.* It helps the clarity of your presentation if each slide has a short heading, showing to which part of the presentation it belongs. One way of doing this can be illustrated with the example presentation structure from Fig. 12.1. The corresponding slides can be given headings like "Background (1)", "Background (2)", "Conclusions", etc. This helps the audience to keep track of what aspect of the project you are talking about at a particular moment. However, this is not to say that all slides must have such headings. In some cases, you may for example want to emphasise a very important point or result by mentioning it in the heading. On the other hand, using "free naming" of slides throughout the whole presentation can result in a somewhat confusing and unstructured impression.
- *Tool use.* Hand written slides can be as clear and nice to read as those written using a software tool, but one of the problems with them is that they are difficult to change. For presentation of numerical results in the form of graphs, using a software tool is essential.
- *Notes or manuscript.* Think beforehand about what to say, so that you will not spend time during the presentation thinking about the phrases and words to use.

How detailed a manuscript you need generally depends on how used you are to giving oral presentations. If this is your first time, you may have to write down almost word for word what you are going to say. If you have lots of experience of giving oral presentations, then you will know already what level of detail you need in your notes or manuscript. Perhaps you can even speak freely without any notes at all, but in all cases, it is necessary to practise the talk, either by yourself or in front of someone else. If you are uncertain about the wording in difficult passages, make sure you write down or memorize those, so that you will not get stuck and loose time during the presentation.

- *Overuse of notes during the presentation.* Notes and manuscripts should mainly be used before the presentation, rather than during it. They are for practising, so that you will know your talk well enough to be able to give it without such aides. It is very boring to listen to a talk where the speaker reads from his or her notes. However, it is fine to occasionally glance at your notes if you forget some key words or phrases. So, the point is not that it is "forbidden" to look at your notes, but that you should only need to look at them occasionally. This is of course achieved by rehearsing.

12.1.2   The Presentation

You should begin any presentation by introducing yourself, the title of your talk, and the name of your supervisor. This introduction should always be short, since it is the content of the project that is the centre of attention, so keep the introduction down to one or two sentences. It is nice to have a title page of your slides that shows the same information, and to show this slide for enough time for the audience to read it. This way, you are clearly signalling the start of your presentation and that the audience should start paying attention to your talk.

A common way of beginning, after the title page, is to show a slide with a list of contents for the talk. However, for short talks, it may be argued that this is a waste of valuable time. The first minute of the talk may actually be the only time when you have the full attention of everybody in the audience. Therefore, it is a good idea to start with important information immediately. If you do decide to use a contents list, make sure that it has items that are meaningful. Starting a 15-min talk by saying that the rest of the talk will consist of: 'introduction followed by background, problems and conclusion', is not very meaningful. Make sure that you state the most important things about your project in the first minutes of the presentation. As you have probably noticed during lectures, it is sometimes difficult to keep listening with full attention for a long time. If you begin your talk by being vague, unclear or simply uninteresting, parts of the audience will almost certainly stop paying attention, which means they will miss the well-formulated arguments that you present later in your talk.

General guidelines:

- *Talk to the audience.* Avoid talking to the floor, to the wall or to the projector screen. Try to keep contact with your audience. Seek eye contact with your supervisor, examiner or even your friends who are listening. But also do so without staring at anyone. During the talk you will of course have to face the projector screen sometimes, for example to point out details shown on the slides.
- *Show the slides properly.* Avoid showing a slide for just a second or two before going on to the next one. In most cases, there is no way that anybody in the audience will grasp the information on your slide within seconds. It is easy to overestimate the speed at which people can grasp the information. You may have spent a long time writing, revising and thinking about the contents of a particular slide, and therefore the information on it may seem obvious to you. The audience, on the other hand, is seeing it for the first time, and they need some time to read and interpret it.
- *Explain things.* For each slide you have to explain clearly to the audience what it shows. If, for example, the slide contains a line graph, you have to tell the audience what the x and y-axes represent (always include legends for all figures and graphs on your slides). Otherwise, the graph is meaningless to look at. Do not expect the audience to find out things for themselves by reading the slide.
- *Avoid reading word by word from the slide.* This should be done only occasionally, when the slide contains, for example, a very important definition, or a quote that is fundamental for your work and very important to communicate exactly to the audience. Otherwise, you should not treat the slides as part of your manuscript. Normally, your slide should contain short phrases ("New method improved results by 20%"), whereas your talk should be more explanatory ("I found in my experiment that the new method, when compared with the current standard, improved the results on this test case by 20%. This was certainly a pleasing result since it fulfilled my first objective.").
- *Keep an eye on the time.* Use your allocated time well. If you have, for example, 20 min for your talk, then practice the talk so that you know how long each part takes. Also leave a margin, so that you don't find yourself running out of time and having to skip some parts. If you do run out of time during the talk, you may have to jump directly to the slide that conclude your talk when there is a minute or so left of the allotted time.
- *Monitor the tempo.* Do not talk too fast, or too slowly. Perhaps you can ask your supervisor beforehand to give you signals as to whether you are talking too fast or too slowly. You can vary the tempo and your voice during the talk in order to emphasise certain things in the presentation.
- *Use a glass of water.* If you get uncertain or nervous during your talk, it can be a good idea to have some form of distraction. The act of reaching for a glass of water, for example, serves as a useful mini break. The audience might think that you are just sipping water for a couple of seconds, but during these few, but valuable seconds, you have time to calm down, soothe the dry throat, and even think

through, for example, how to introduce the next slide or give a good answer to a question from the audience.

- *Do not block the view.* Find a convenient place were you can stand, so that you do not block the projected slides. This issue of not blocking the view is also of importance if you are using transparencies and an overhead projector. When pointing to figures etc., it is generally better to point to the projection screen rather than to the transparency on the projector.
- *Use a pointing device.* Think beforehand about how you will point to things on your slides if you need to. This is particularly important if you are using transparencies, where pointing at the slide itself would force you to look right into the light of the projector, so that when you look back up again you can only see black spots. A better method is to use a laser pointer or a stick. If you use a laser pointer, the time to find out how it works is before the talk, rather than during it. If you use a stick, try to avoid showing your nervousness by swinging it back and forth or otherwise jiggling it. Unless you use it very often, put it down on the desk when you do not need it.

No matter how well you have prepared beforehand, do not be surprised if you feel a bit nervous at the beginning of the presentation. This is normal, and happens to almost everybody, no matter how many times they have given presentations before. If the nervousness is so bad that it really troubles you, it may help to remember the examiner and the rest of the audience are interested in your project, and not in whether you are nervous or not. If the content of your talk is of high quality, then a trembling voice or shaky fingers are of no consequence, and may not even be noticed by anyone.

12.1.3   What to Say

What to include in your presentation depends simply on what is required by the department, examiner or supervisor, or whoever is expecting you to deliver a presentation. You should therefore find out the requirements and expectations they have, before beginning to structure and plan your presentation. When giving a presentation at the very end of the project, you should usually cover the whole project, and give a complete presentation beginning with background and aims, and finishing with conclusions and future work. Other presentations, given earlier in the process, can have other requirements, like focusing on the problem description or on the choice of methods. Again, find these requirements out by speaking to your supervisor or examiner, before structuring and planning the presentation.

Given the things you need to include in your presentation, the main difficulty will usually be to fit the material and the message into the allotted time. There is always a lot that needs to be explained, and the time to explain it is short. The key goal to keep in mind is to try to be *precise* and *concise*. Being precise in what you say helps the audience understand it more quickly, which means that you can explain more material in a given time. Being concise is a matter of planning the presentation well so that you find the briefest possible way of expressing your message, without losing any clarity.

If you know that your project has some weaknesses then it is usually better to be open and honest about this in your presentation. Attempts to try to hide weaknesses or deficiencies is unlikely to fool the examiner, since he/she is actively looking for those, and usually has a lot of experience in doing so. Also, examiners often have discussions with supervisors to gain additional information. So the examiner may know more about the project than is available in the report and presentation. We believe that openly presenting mistakes is usually a better approach, both from the point of view of maintaining integrity as well as showing that you have the insight to understand that you have made mistakes. If, in addition, you can also demonstrate what you have learnt from a mistake, then you will most likely score additional points in the examiner's record book.

12.1.4 Handling Questions

The defence is your chance to show that you know your own work so well that you can defend it when difficult and critical questions are asked about it. If you have done your work well, this part will be easy, since you will have spent so much time on your project that you know much more about it than anyone else.

However, all projects have some weak points along with the strong ones. This means that there will be things in your project that can be criticised – and should be criticised, so that the project can be evaluated as objectively as possible.

Advice on how to handle questions:

- *Be as clear as possible in your replies.* Remember that the opponent is not only asking the questions for himself or herself. There is normally an audience listening to the presentation, and at least there is your examiner who is listening attentively to your replies. The audience has not normally had any chance to read your report, and therefore needs more explanation than the opponent. In other words, clear answers are needed, so that the defence does not become an "internal" debate between you and the opponent excluding the audience at large.
- *Clarify the question if necessary.* If you are in the least bit uncertain about what the opponent is asking, then make sure that the question is clarified before you attempt to answer it. Either ask the opponent to clarify the question, or rephrase the question as you have interpreted it, and ask the opponent if that is what he or she had in mind.
- *Do not take criticism personally.* It is the project that is being questioned, and not your competence or intelligence. Try to be objective and admit mistakes if there really are some flaws in your project. If you have some sufficiently strong points, you can emphasise these and safely admit the mistakes. No project is perfect anyway.

- *Get your point across.* Unlike the presentation, which you plan and organise to get across the main points of your work, the defence is more in the hands of the opponent. It is the opponent's prerogative to choose which questions to ask, and therefore to choose what parts of your work to focus on. However, it is still possible to make sure that the main points of your work are communicated to the audience and the examiner. You cannot do this by choosing to ignore or pretending to "misunderstand" the question, or by only talking about what you want to talk about. Rather, keep in mind what the main points are that you want to communicate, and when you are asked questions on other topics, you might be able to see how they relate to your main points. You can then argue for this connection in your reply.
- *Do not try to avoid answering the question.* If the reply to a "tricky" question reveals a weakness in your project, then answer to that effect anyway. Otherwise your examiner will realise that, not only is there a flaw in the project, but you are trying to hide it by evading the question! This is would just make things worse.
- *Do not brush off the question as irrelevant.* You may very well get questions that you consider truly irrelevant to your project, given its aims and objectives. However, merely replying by saying that the question is irrelevant is not sufficient. If the opponent asks a particular question, then he or she believes it to be relevant. You must then reply by providing your arguments for why you think it is irrelevant. These arguments can be based on the aim you have chosen, but it is necessary to keep in mind that you could have chosen other aims. Merely replying that "this is outside the scope of my project" is not usually sufficient. You also have to defend the scope that you chose.
- *Do not retaliate.* If you feel that the opponent is asking questions in an overly aggressive or negative way, try to keep calm and act with dignity. Remember that the examiner is also scrutinising the behaviour of your opponent. If an opponent is obviously unfair, you may actually gain more sympathy from the examiner. Retaliating with snide remarks, however, will generally not do you any good.
- *Prepare.* The defence is one of the most important events during your project, since it may influence the examiner's impression of your work. It is perfectly possible that an examiner, who has so far been happy with your work, discovers weak points during the defence which he or she had not thought of before. Similarly, an examiner who has been very critical of your work to date, may be influenced by your strong arguments presented in the defence to change his or her mind about the grade. For these reasons, it is necessary to prepare for the defence. This point is so important that it has been assigned a section of its own.

12.1.5 *Preparing for the Defence*

It may seem as if the defence is difficult to prepare, since you do not know which questions will be asked of you. However, it is possible to prepare for it by imagining that you are the opponent of your own work. In other words, read your own report using the guidelines for opponents (see Sect. 12.2.2), and keep notes of the questions that arise. This should give you a set of questions, to which you can subsequently begin to prepare answers. There is of course no guarantee that you will come up with the same questions as your opponent, but it is likely that there will be a significant overlap between the opponent's list of questions and yours. In addition, during this procedure you will read and scrutinise your report carefully, which is a key ingredient in preparing for the defence.

One problem with preparing for the defence is that you may have been working with great focus and intensity on your project for a long time. As a result, certain questions and problems will be very much at the centre of your attention. The opponent, however, is reading the report for the first time, and may have a very different perspective from yours. While you are focused on some detailed aspect of the problem, you may be missing some more high-level aspects, such as how the work in general fits into the subject area, or how it compares with an alternative research orientation. In short, your focus may be too narrow, so that your opponent's questions surprise you by being more general than you had expected.

One of the best remedies for the problem of focusing too narrowly is to take the writing of the future work section seriously. This is a part of the report that is sometimes neglected. The writing of it takes place at the end of the project – when the discussion of whether aims and objectives have been met is finished, when perhaps your energy is running low, and when your focus is already on the presentation and defence. Taking the writing of the future work section seriously is a good way of preparing for the defence. This section serves the purpose of placing the work within a wider context and showing its usefulness. Thus, it provides you with some answers to questions of a more general nature.

Another remedy for the problem of being too narrowly focused is to try to find some time, just before you start preparing for the defence, when you step away from your work and not think about it. You might afterwards see your work in a different light, and thereby be more likely to assess it in similar ways to your opponent.

Another useful way of preparing for the defence is to have your supervisor ask you a number of questions. This has the advantage that the supervisor can evaluate your replies and give some tips for improvements. For the method to work properly, it is important to prepare for the practice defence as thoroughly as for the real defence. Coming poorly prepared to the practice defence can result in nervousness from not being able to answer the supervisor's questions.

Although your supervisor is experienced and knowledgeable, it is impossible for him or her to predict all the questions that the opponent will ask. So, if a practice defence is used as part of the preparations, remember that completely different questions may be asked at the actual defence.

If the method of having a practice defence is not used, a good alternative is to have a discussion with your supervisor where you make an assessment of strong and weak points in the project. You can then discuss how the strong points can best be formulated and brought into the discussion during the defence, as well as how the project can be defended despite its weak points.

As part of your preparations for the defence, you may want to document some of your arguments. For example, you may want to make some extra slides of material which is not included in the presentation, but which answers questions that you think are very likely to be asked. Keep in mind, however, that this work is somewhat wasted if the particular questions are not asked, so it is not advisable to spend too much time making "backup" presentation slides. In addition, some examiners may disagree with the use of prepared material during the defence – feeling that the student should cope with the defence using verbal arguments only.

12.2   Acting as Opponent

Next we give some guidelines on how to act as an opponent, and how to prepare for opposition. Note that the opponent could be either a student or the examiner, and the guidelines are applicable for both.

12.2.1   How to Act as Opponent

To know how to behave as an opponent, it is useful to think about what the purpose of the defence-opposition part of a presentation is. The point is that the presented work should be examined critically, so that the arguments presented by the speaker can be tested in a discussion. The opponent asks questions which the presenter should answer, so that the examiner can judge whether the presenter can defend the work. If the presenter can reply successfully with good arguments, this generally convinces the examiner that the work is solid and can withstand critical examination.

However, this does not mean that the opponent should ask questions that are critical in a negative sense, i.e. the opponent should not simply criticise the work. The fact is that no matter how solid and good a project is, it is relatively easy to find something negative to say about it. Rather, the opponent should think of the questions as having the purpose, not of criticising, but of testing the strength and solidity of the presenter's arguments. In other words, acting as opponent does not mean that you should hope to "win" a "battle" by being mean or aggressive. If you ask a difficult question, and the presenter returns with an excellent, insightful and intelligent answer, then you as opponent should think of that as a successful outcome. You have done your job and asked a good question, and the fact that the presenter also had a good answer is good for him or her. In addition, it is also good for you and the audience since you have all gained a new perspective on the presented work.

Another pitfall of acting as opponent is that it is easy to fall into a pattern where one merely tries to show off one's own intelligence and deep understanding of the work, rather than asking relevant questions. It is therefore important to keep in mind that the purpose is to test the presenter's knowledge. The questions should be short, direct and to the point, so that no time is wasted. As much time as possible should be devoted to the presenter spelling out the arguments in defence of the work.

To be able to ask good questions, it is necessary to read the whole report very carefully, and prepare a set of questions beforehand. Some tips for how this can be done are listed in Sect. 12.2.2. However, the fact that you have all the questions prepared beforehand does not mean that you should keep to those questions solely. It is also necessary to listen very attentively to the presentation. Quite often, something that was unclear in the report becomes clarified during the presentation, so that questions can be dropped from the prepared list. It is useful to keep this in mind while preparing, and to add more questions than you think there will be time to ask, so that you have some "backup" questions to replace those that are answered in the presentation.

12.2.2   Preparing for Opposition

Here follows a set of guidelines for how a report can be scrutinised, in preparation for the opposition. The guidelines follow approximately the same order as most reports are structured (see Chap. 14 for a discussion of report structure). The guidelines consist of a set of questions that can be useful for the opponent to ask while reading the report. The list is obviously not complete, but includes questions on the most important aspects to consider.

Problem statement

- Has the author explained the problem that is to be investigated in a clear and understandable way?
- Has the author provided convincing arguments for the need to investigate this problem?
- Has the author provided convincing arguments that conducting the investigation will lead to the possibility of obtaining a solution, or increasing our understanding of the problem domain?

Aims and objectives

- Has the author identified a specific aim to be achieved in the project?
- Is the identified aim explained in a clear and understandable way?
- Has the author derived a list of specific objectives from the aim?
- Are the objectives presented in a clear and structured way?
- Do the objectives support the aim, i.e. will fulfilling all the objectives lead to the aim being achieved?

Methods

- Has the author clearly identified and explained the methods that could potentially be used in the investigation?
- Has the author provided an insightful discussion of advantages and disadvantages of each potential method for the investigation?

- Has the author clearly stated which method (or methods) was selected for the investigation?
- Has the author provided convincing arguments for the selected method(s)?
- Has the author described clearly how the selected method(s) will be applied?

Data

- Has the author presented the collected data in a clear, understandable, systematic and correct way?
- Is the collected data sufficient, given the stated aims and objectives of the project?

Analysis

- Has the author made a thorough and systematic analysis of the data obtained?
- Is the analysis described in a clear and understandable way?
- If the data are quantitative, has the author applied significance tests or other numerical evaluation techniques in a relevant and correct way?
- Has the author evaluated the stated aims and objectives in the light of the data obtained?

Conclusions

- Has the author provided conclusions that are relevant, given the stated aims and objectives?
- If the work contains one or more hypotheses, does the author draw conclusions about whether these hypotheses are supported or falsified by the results?
- Has the author provided valid arguments for the stated conclusions?

Discussion and future work

- Has the author discussed the work in an insightful way, and thereby placed the work into a wider context?
- Has the author identified relevant and plausible continuations of the work?

Overall assessment

- Were the objectives of the project fulfilled?
- Was the aim of the project reached?
- Has the project furthered our understanding of the problem investigated?
- Will this work be useful in the future?
- Is the report well structured and understandable?
- Is the report well written?

Additional questions

- Does the author have a critical viewpoint, i.e. have sources used in the work been critically evaluated by the author?
- Have terms of importance to the report been clearly defined?
- Is the use of terms and definitions consistent throughout the report?

- Is it clear when something is the author's own work, and when it is someone else's work?
- Have all sources used by the author been clearly identified by use of literature references, and have the references been made in a correct way?
- Are you aware of any additional relevant literature on the topic, which has not been used and cited by the author?
- Are you aware of any work which closely resembles the work done in the project, but which has not been identified by the author?

12.3 Prepare the Final Version of your Report

Depending on the rules in your department (and possibly on the outcome of the defence), you may or may not have an opportunity to revise your report after the defence. In such cases, when preparing the final version of your report, you can make improvements by considering comments received from your supervisor, your examiner and your opponent. In addition, you may have already identified sections in the report that could be improved. It is useful to make a list of all major potential adjustments and decide, if possible together with your supervisor, which adjustments should be made and which should not be considered for the final version of the report.

Remember that the report is a "living" document, i.e. any changes that you introduce at this point can affect other sections or chapters in your report. You should read your own report as carefully as if you were reading it as an opponent.

Finally, it is also worthwhile to check the examination criteria one more time.

Part III
Supplements

13
Information-Seeking and Use

Throughout this book it has been mentioned that you will necessarily have to search for information at various stages in the process of planning and writing your thesis project. In this chapter we will take a closer look at the practice of information seeking and use. The chapter employs a perspective that is grounded in the idea that the information seeking process is improved if the seeker has a general and reflective picture of what he or she is actually involved in when he or she is engaged in an information practice. Therefore some parts of this chapter are used for brief descriptions of information seeking models and theories. It should be pointed out that the term information practice is deliberately chosen since it denotes an activity that is more than a mere sequence of tasks being performed with the purpose of finding information. The term practice can be described as a conscious system for achieving certain goals, serving certain functions, producing certain results (Marton, 2000, 231).

13.1 Information Literacy for Computer Science

A widely spread concept that is used to describe the competence and skills involved in information seeking and use is information literacy. It is debated whether a person can develop a general, or generic, information literacy. In this book the standpoint is that information literacy should be seen as a competence that is being developed in connection to a particular discipline. Research is conducted in different ways in different fields. Thus, this chapter deals with the information literate computer science student. According to this standpoint the information literate computer science student needs to develop a familiarity with the computer science domain. Another way to put it is to say that the computer science student needs to be aware of the particular conventions (unspoken or outspoken) that exist in the computer science domain. From an information-seeking perspective a domain, or a discipline, could be described by the research questions that can be asked within the domain, by the resources researchers consult to find information, and the channels they use to disseminate their findings and results. Developing this kind of understanding for the specific research discipline is not something that is done over night; it is something

M. Berndtsson et al. (eds.), *Thesis Projects: A Guide for Students in Computer Science and Information Systems.*
© Springer 2008

that more or less slowly develops during frequent interaction with the computer science literature, the information sources used, and with active researchers within the discipline.

13.2   Information Searching, Seeking, and Behaviour

To help us understand contextual aspects of information-related practices it might be helpful to visualize the processes of searching for and using information as in Fig. 13.1.

As the figure implies one can conceptualize information-related practices as consisting of three layers:

1. Information searching – the performance of an activity such as interacting with a computer-based system, with the aim of finding information.
2. Information seeking – often described as a process during which the seeker not only searches for information but also makes decisions about which information sources to use and evaluates already found information.
3. Information behaviour – all human behaviour, passive or active, in relation to information and information sources.

At the core of the model we find the activity of actual information searching, which could be exemplified with the concrete task of searching for information through, for example, interaction with a computer, e.g. searching a bibliographic database such as a library catalogue. During your project you will most likely find yourself in front of a computer a number of times trying to find useful documents by searching various databases. These sessions – during which you use tools such as catalogues, libraries, the web, databases etc – taken together form what in Fig. 13.1 has been

Fig. 13.1   A nested model of conceptual areas, adapted from (Wilson, 1999, 840)

labelled the process of information seeking. The information seeking process also contains stages where you do not actually perform information searches. For instance you will need to plan and think through your search session, define your information needs, decide what information sources you will use, and so forth. An information search session will (hopefully) lead to a result that consists of lists of references, including abstracts, i.e. short summaries of the actual articles. These are the initial objects of evaluation and judgment: by studying the abstracts you can make decisions on whether you actually think the article is of value to you. You may not fully evaluate or judge your search results in connection to the actual search session; hence the information seeking process consists of several activities: planning your information search sessions, carrying out the searches (information searching), evaluating the results of search, and (based on the outcome) planning additional searches.

Judging and evaluating has to do with one of the key elements of information use; that is the element that deals with selection and rejection of information. It is not always easy to evaluate for example an article on the basis of a 200 word abstract. The evaluation activity is connected to the issue of relevance, which is a term that can be understood in more than one way. For instance one can think in terms of topical relevance, which probably is the most common way to think of relevance. But it could also be so that a document is relevant from a "paradigmatic" perspective: The most relevant texts are not necessarily about the subject or topic the you are doing your research on, but offers a way of thinking about and approaching the subject (Talja, 2002).

According to our experience novice information seekers very often think of relevance only as "topical", and therefore tend to be too fast in rejecting documents that could be useful for developing an approach for how to deal with a particular research problem.

When you are in the midst of a thesis project you will probably note that the work starts to absorb you, so to speak. It is likely that you think of your work during many of the hours of the day. When you are very focused on a specific task, like a thesis project, it is also likely that you pay attention to things that relate to your work, for example when talking to other people and when reading other texts that do not deal with your subject. There are many testimonies in the literature about researchers and other information seekers that "accidentally" find useful information. This is an aspect that can be said to deal with the outer circle in Fig. 13.1., information behaviour; a concept that has been described as "the totality of human behaviour in relation to sources and channels of information, including both active and passive information seeking, and information use" (Wilson, 2000).

13.2.1 Search Techniques

In the section above it was stated that information searching could be described as the concrete task of searching for information through, for example, interaction with a computer. In the next section we will take a more detailed look at how a bibliographic database can be used efficiently. It should be mentioned, however, that the process of information searching can be performed in different ways. It is reasonable to assume that many people think of information searching as the act of typing a few words into the search box of a web based search engine with the expectation to retrieve documents that contain these words, but the field of information searching can also be widened and include what we call browsing. If we stay in the web environment, browsing could be described as the act of following links between web pages and web sites in order to find information.

In a library, the search would be performed by using the library catalogue to search for documents by a particular author, or with a particular title, or on a certain subject. If we instead decided to browse for documents in a library, we would rather go to the shelves and let the eye run along the spines of the books in order to find the "right" title. We could also browse through tables of content in journals in order to find articles. The last technique that shall be mentioned is sometimes called "chaining" or "footnote chasing", and is performed by following references in one document to another. It is not unusual for an experienced computer science researcher (or any other researcher) to start examining an article or a book by browsing through the reference list. If one is familiar with a particular research field one can probably tell a lot about an article by noticing who the author have cited. There are actually certain databases – or citation indexes – that allow researchers to trace connections between authors and between articles by providing answers to questions such as who cited this work and how often has this work been cited. A well known source for this kind of information is the *Science Citation Index*.

The concluding remark for this section on search techniques is that it is worth to reflect on which technique is most suitable for a particular purpose – sometimes it might be better to search, whereas on other occasions it is more appropriate with browsing or chaining.

13.3   A Session with INSPEC

In what follows we will take a look at the bibliographic database INSPEC, which is one of many databases that can be useful for you in connection to your thesis project. It is likely that you will have to consult a number of different databases to find the information you need for your work, since no single database contains all the information you need. However, even though there are numerous different databases within the computer science discipline alone, there are certain features that tend to reappear in many of them. So, by looking at INSPEC as an example, we hope to say something not only about this particular database but also about how to search bibliographic databases in general.

That some databases have the prefix *bibliographic* means that they record information in the form of texts, in contrast to for example numeric information. In short,

INSPEC contains detailed descriptions of documents. These descriptions will help you not only to find out what has been published on a particular subject, they will also provide you with the details you need to obtain the documents that are of interest to you.

A bibliographic database is commonly provided by a database provider – or vendor – often a commercial company that specializes in information provision. INSPEC can for example be obtained from at least seven different information providers. The provider is not necessarily the same as the producer of the database. These matters, though, are nothing that you need to think very much about. Normally it is the university library that provides the university with access to a range of databases and accordingly also makes the deals with the information providers.

In our example INSPEC is provided by the information provider SilverPlatter who delivers the database with their certain interface and features. It might be so that you have experience from using INSPEC at another institution where it was provided by another vendor, which means that the features of the interface may have been different from the ones of SilverPlatter. However, it is still the same database; the content is the same but it is presented and displayed in a different way.

13.3.1   What will you Find?

INSPEC is a reference database. It contains detailed references to documents, but not the documents themselves. There are, however, also some records through which you can find external links to the documents. A reference database is different from a full text database, that also contains the documents that the references refer to. Amongst the document types that you will find references to in INSPEC are books and book-chapters, dissertations, reports, journal articles, and conference papers. INSPEC is produced by the Institution of Engineering and Technology, which is a professional society. The database has been developed over decades and contains approximately nine million records. Around 500,000 records are added annually. Computer science is not the only field that is covered by INSPEC, it also covers subjects such as electronics and engineering.

13.3.2   Boolean Commands

To learn how to efficiently use a bibliographic database it is necessary that you have general knowledge about the Boolean search commands AND, OR, and NOT. Using Boolean search commands allows you to narrow down your search by using special terms before and/or between your terms (see Fig. 13.2).

Let us take a look at a few examples. If you type the following search string into the search box:

Boolean team	*For what purpose*
AND	To make sure a term is included
OR	To include alternative terms
NOT	To exclude term(s)

Fig. 13.2 Boolean commands

- Computing AND visualization

You increase the chance that what you find is about computerized visualization. To ensure that you capture both ways of spelling a specific term you can formulate a search string such as:

- Visualization OR visualization

By typing:

- Visualization NOT drawing

You decrease the risk for including documents about visualization through drawing (by hand).

Our examples provide us with the opportunity to present yet another plausible way of combining terms with Boolean commands, in a more refined example:

- Computing AND (visualisation OR visualization)

This example points out that in case you want to combine more than two terms and include different Boolean commands in the same search string, then it is necessary to use brackets to group the parts of the search string in a functional way.

You may have noticed that the Boolean commands function in a similar manner to + and − that you perhaps use when you search the web with a search engine.

As in most databases Boolean commands can be typed manually into the search box in INSPEC. But there is also an option that lets you use the commands by choosing them from menus, which is a feature that many searchers find useful.

13.3.3 *Information Structure*

Basic knowledge about how the bibliographic information is structured in the database will help you improve both searching the database and reading the information the database provides you with. The bibliographic information is presented in a structured and standardized way, which means that every record has a similar look to it, even though the information that each record contains is unique. The records are structured according to certain fields. Each field contains a certain kind of bibliographic information. Thus, information about authors is found in the author-field, title information in the title-field, etc. From an information searching perspective some fields are more interesting than others. Familiarity with the following fields will most likely improve your ability to search for information in INSPEC (note that the abbreviations used in the list are the same as those used in the database):

- *AB – Abstract*. contains a short summary of the original document.
- *AU – Author*. contains the name(s) of the individual(s) responsible for the intellectual content of the original document.
- *DE – Descriptors*. contains standardized terms from a set list of index terms. Terms can also be phrases, i.e. contain more than a single word. When searching for phrases they shall be hyphenated (for example decision-making).
- *ID – Identifiers*. contains free-language words and phrases assigned by INSPEC indexers. Identifiers are generated from the title, abstract, full text of the article, and from the indexer's specialized knowledge. They give a more detailed description of the relevant content of the document than provided by the original title or by the abstract.
- *IS – ISSN*. contains the International Standard Serial Number (ISSN) of the original periodical described in the record. Every periodical publication, such as a journal, has its own unique serial number. This number can be very useful when you are trying to locate a particular publication.
- *SO – Source*. contains the bibliographic citation for original documents. The bibliographic citation provides you with details about the title of the publication that the text was published in, the publication year, volume, issue number and pages.
- *SU – Subject Terms*. enables you to search in the Descriptors (DE) and Identifiers (ID) fields simultaneously.
- *TI – Title*. contains the title of the original document.

To be able to utilize your familiarity with the various fields you also need to know that it is possible to formulate queries that combine terms that appear in different fields. Like most bibliographic databases, INSPEC offers the user more than one search interface. Here you will be introduced to three different interfaces. It is likely that the first interface you meet is the most basic or simple interface, so let us start with that. It contains just one search box into which you can type the term(s) you want to use for your search. The basic search interface also gives you the opportunity to use a drop down-menu to specify in which field you want the term(s) to appear.

For example: a simple search for the terms *interactive* AND *multimedia* without any specification about where the terms are supposed to appear in the record will produce a result with nearly eight thousand records. To refine your query and thus be more detailed about what you are looking for, you can take advantage of the advanced search interface. Here you can type your terms into separate boxes. Each box is paired with a scroll down-menu. At this stage you can also decide how you want the boxes to relate to each other, by choosing from the suggested Boolean commands. If you chose to type the term *interactive* in the first box and the term *multimedia* in the second box, you will also have the opportunity to specify where you want each term to appear in the record by choosing a particular field in the drop down-menu. If you also choose to click the radio-button that connects the two boxes with the Boolean command AND, it will result in a search string that can be described like this:

- *interactive* IN SU [the term must appear within the subject term-field] AND *multimedia* IN ID [the term must appear within the identifiers-field]

Even if this search string does not result in a very precise list of records, it is worth noticing that the amount of hits compared with the search we performed with the basic interface is reduced by 50%. This could be said to be an effective way of reducing the number of records that your query will result in. It is also a way of finding records that refer to texts that are about the subject you want to know more about, but do not have titles that match the terms that you use.

Very often even a query produced in the advanced interface needs to be refined further. That could be done in many ways. Most queries can be narrowed by thinking through the information need at least one more time. In this case – about interactive multimedia – you could ask yourself: am I interested in interactive multimedia in a particular setting or context? Could I relate any particular user group to my interest? Very often this kind of further questioning results in more focused terms. Most search sessions are more time consuming than expected. A variety of terms and combinations of terms need to be tested. The advanced search interface only allows the searcher to combine three (or less) different terms. That brings us to the third interface that shall be presented here, the search history-interface.

The search history-interface can be used for different reasons. Since the search history contains documentation about all the queries you have performed during a session it can help you to remember which terms, and combinations of terms, you have used. But the search history-interface also allows you to extend a search string, to build upon an already performed query, or to combine two or more different queries.

If the first of the two following queries does not result in a satisfactory list of hits you can chose to extend it by adding yet another term. It would then look like the second query in the subsequent list.

1 *interactive* in su AND *multimedia* in id
2 #1 AND *computer-games*

The last of the above examples should be interpreted as query number one (which in INSPEC as well as in many other bibliographic databases is symbolized with the sign #) being combined with the term *computer-games*.

It is common that you have to try numerous combinations before reaching satisfactory results, which may take some time. Many databases, like INSPEC, allow you to save your search history, so that you can upload it the next time you start a session. You will thereby be able to continue where you ended the earlier session.

In this section you have been introduced to three different interfaces. Especially by using the advanced interface – combined with extended searches performed via the search history-interface – you will most likely be able to find a lot of useful references. Before entering the next section it should be mentioned that there are more ways to use INSPEC effectively. For example, searches can be performed by using features such as the index and thesaurus.

13.3.4 How to Get Hold of Documents

When you find a reference of interest in a reference database you will need to take yet another step in order to obtain the actual document. This can be done in a number of ways. Occasionally you will find references that lead to documents that are freely available on the web. Most often, however, you will have to search the university library to see whether the document is available there. To find out if the document that you are looking for is available for free on the web. it is a good idea to work with more than one window open at the same time; one for searching the bibliographic database, and one for, let's say, Google which you can use for finding out if the document is available on the web. By copying a document title found in the database and pasting it into Google you will in a quick and easy manner find out if it is available for free.

In case you do find a document which is freely available on the web, it is important to be aware of the fact that some papers can be published in different versions. Authors some times publish drafts or early versions of their work. To find out if the text that you have found has been published in a journal it is a good idea to look for publication details such as the journal title, issue and volume numbers, page numbers and publication year. It is also common to find information about submission date and date for acceptance in connection to an article that has been published in a journal, see Fig. 13.3.

That kind of information would not appear in a draft or pre-print version of an article.

Most university libraries provide their users with a list or a searchable database that contains all the periodicals the library subscribes to. These lists most often let you search for titles of periodicals, but they do not allow you to search for specific articles within these publications. This means that you will have to think of your search for a specific article as consisting of two steps. The first step is to find out if the library has the publication that "your" article was published in. Searching the periodical list for the ISSN of the publication you are looking for is an efficient way to find out if the publication is available via the library. One could of course also search for the name of the publication, but there are publications with very similar

Received 20 August 2005; received in revised form 2 February 2006; accepted 15 February 2006

Fig. 13.3 Information about submission, revision and acceptance is often available on the title page of journal articles

titles, and even sometimes the same title. Once you have found the publication you are looking for you have to find the actual article. The information you need to do this is presented in the source field in the bibliographic information found in, in our example, INSPEC. There you will find details such as publication year, volume, issue and page numbers. Nowadays the majority of scientific journals are available in electronic versions, which means that you probably will be able to print out "your" article. Occasionally, though, there is only a physical "paper-version" of the publication you are looking for. In those cases there is a third step involved in the localization process: you will have to find the physical space for the publication within the library.

After this account of the session with INSPEC, we will return to the greater picture and take a further look at the information seeking-process.

13.4   The Information Seeking-Process

The concept of information behaviour implies that information-related activities should not be seen as solely rational. There is evidence that the information seeker often experiences feelings such as confusion, frustration and doubt. Many students experience that it can be helpful to be aware of this when they are engaged in a research project.

The information seeking process (ISP) is often described as consisting of various stages. A widely spread visualization has been developed by the American researcher Carol Kuhlthau, (see Table 13.1). The unique feature of this particular model is that it takes into consideration the affective aspects that where mentioned above.

As can be seen in the table above there is a variety of feelings that might occur during the ISP. Many novice information seekers seem to suffer from what has been

Table 13.1   Model of the information seeking process, adapted from (Kuhlthau, 1993, 43)

Stages	Task Initiation	Topic Selection	Prefocus Exploration	Focus Formulation	Information Collection	Search Closure	Starting writing
Feelings	Uncertainty	optimism	confusion/ frustra- tion	clarity	cense of direction/ confidence	relief	satisfaction or dissatis- faction
Thoughts	ambiguity	—————————————————————————→			specificity		
				increased	interest ————————→		
Actions	seeking relevant information	————————————————————→				seeking pertinent informa- tion	

called the uncertainty principle, which means that they often tend to abandon their original ideas when they experience the stage that in the model is labeled pre-focus exploration. At that point it is not unusual that the seeker decides to change his or her subject of study, due to the feelings of confusion, frustration and doubt that might arise in connection to the ISP.

It is interesting to note that in Kuhlthau's model the information seeking process also contains the stages of task initiation, topic selection and starting writing, which implies that the process of information seeking is intertwined with the process of carrying out the thesis project. Even though this particular depiction of the information seeking process invites to an interpretation of the process as rather linear, it is important to acknowledge the iterative aspects of the process. There are other models of the ISP that emphasize its non-linear aspects. For example the ISP has been described as analogue with an artist's palette where all the colors are available all the time (Foster, 2004).

13.5   Two Basic Strategies for Information Seeking

Many students find it difficult to identify the core in the literature of their chosen subject. The matter of defining the scope for the investigation often causes trouble. According to Kuhlthau (1993), a common problem for information seeking students is to formulate a focus. Often this problem is caused by the fact that the information seeker is too eager to engage in the process of information seeking, so eager so that he or she does not take the necessary time to plan and carefully define the task. We could say that to define the core in the literature one needs to "get close to", or learn more about, the chosen subject.

13.5.1   The Concept Map

There are several techniques to "get closer" to the subject. One example is the concept map, which can be used for sharpening the focus of the task, but also for generating useful search terms, and for identifying useful sources of information. Not much is needed to produce a concept map. It is enough with a blank sheet of paper and a pen. The map can concentrate on the whole project, or on separate parts of it. The main idea is to set your thoughts free and by brainstorming try to generate as many relevant aspects of the planned task as possible. All terms and phrases should be written on the paper and eventually grouped according to relations between the concepts. A common result is that you eventually identify different clusters in the map; groups of related concepts that might in themselves be enough for a whole project. Another advantage with the concept map is that the terms and phrases that have been generated often can be used as search terms. It

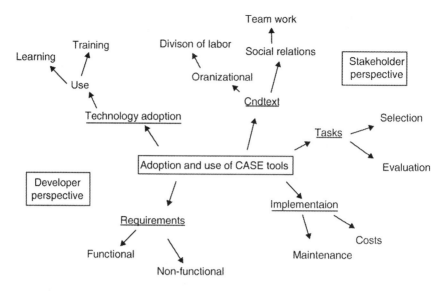

Fig. 13.4   Example concept map

is not uncommon that the information seeker finds it necessary to produce more than one map during the information seeking process. It is a good idea to save the maps since they can provide an overview of the process you have gone through. They can give you a fairly good picture of how you have been thinking during different stages of the process.

Figure 13.4 shows a basic sketch of an example concept map that could be developed around a research problem concerning the adoption and use of CASE tools. This example could of course be developed further. The relations between the different terms are for instance not given per se and could be elaborated, perhaps in another map. The production of a map like this might even result in a decision to further refine the research focus; sometimes it turns out that one single cluster is a big enough area to base your project's problem definition on.

13.5.2   Personal Research Information Management

Another strategic aspect is related to what is often called personal research information management, or PRIM. Over time, even during a project that is relatively limited in time – such as a thesis project – the information seeker tends to generate a lot of information. This information will probably consist of references to documents of all sorts, but it could also be the actual documents – physical or electronic copies of articles and reports, for instance. To have a carefully planned strategy for handling this material can be of great help. There are various ways in which you can structure and manage your personal research information. From the most basic way of keeping documents orderly in marked physical folders, over self-made electronic structures of files and folders, to commercial information management software such as for example EndNote or ProCite. For this text it is enough to state that it is of importance to already from the beginning be aware of the need to keep information in order in a way that allows easy and quick access.

14
The Report

14.1 Introduction

Although this chapter is placed at the end of the book, it does not mean that you should consider the writing of your report as the last step in your project. Rather, writing should be considered a continuous process, carried out throughout the duration of the project. One reason for this is that the report fulfils several purposes. Most importantly, the report represents the means for disseminating results and experiences to other people (it is also a proof of project existence). Writing is also an excellent way of structuring your thoughts. Therefore, writing during the different stages of your project helps you to keep the focus in the project. It also helps you to communicate with your supervisor, and it provides another means for you to get his/her feedback on drafts of different parts of the report while you are working on the project.

When you proofread your writing you should ask yourself, "Have I said what I wanted to say?" If not, you should go back and engage in some redrafting. Becoming a good writer takes a lot of time. The best researchers spend significant time making sure their presentation is excellent, often rewriting sentences and paragraphs numerous times before they are satisfied. This is part of what makes them so good. You should remember that it does not matter how brilliant your work is if it is not being disseminated. Poor writing will undermine your authority in the reader's eyes, and good writing will strengthen it. However, remember that you should always write to be understood, not to impress!

When writing a report, you should communicate the results to the target reader groups as *efficiently* as possible. This means that the language and structure must enable the reader to understand the contents with minimum effort. Efficient communication does not imply anything about the length of the report, since efficient communication is not about the text being short or long.

In any academic project, it is also important that the results are reported truthfully. Hence, all significant results should be included in the report, even if they are unfavourable ones. Remember that the purpose of academic projects is to extend the state-of-the-art knowledge. If only favourable results were reported then we would definitely not have a full understanding of the problem. Thus, it is your responsibility to truthfully and objectively report both expected and unexpected

M. Berndtsson et al. (eds.), *Thesis Projects: A Guide for Students in Computer Science and Information Systems*.
© Springer 2008

results; that is the nature of the scientific voyage and it is the foundation which knowledge is based on.

A common question that many students raise is how long the report should be. A suitable response is, "How short can you make it?" The point is that a report should include only what is necessary, and everything else should be excluded. The report should be concise and focused. There should be enough detail to: (1) follow the chain of thought at an acceptable level of effort; (2) be able to apply the approach and solution to a related problem elsewhere; and (3) verify your results and contribution. If your report does not satisfy these criteria then it is lacking in detail.

Your report is a reflection of your project, and cannot compensate for any deficiencies or errors that result from lack of care in all the previous phases of the project.

This chapter will discuss the target reader group (Sect. 14.2), the requirements on the report (Sect. 14.3), issues that need to be considered when structuring the report (Sect. 14.4), and different styles of reports (Sect. 14.5). The chapter ends with a description of how to manage references (Sect. 14.6).

14.2   Who is the Report for?

Before starting to write your report, you need to decide who is going to read it. It goes without saying that your supervisor and your examiner are going to read it. In fact, your supervisor will read parts of the report several times during your project. However, the report is not necessarily targeted at them. In fact, it is most likely to have multiple reader groups, e.g. fellow students, project collaborators, future employers etc. Having multiple and distinct reader groups does not necessarily mean that the report is going to be more complicated to write with respect to structure and contents, but it certainly becomes a more delicate issue, due to the requirement of ensuring that all the reader groups are satisfied. However, for thesis reports, this is the most important consideration when planning, writing and revising. The reason is obvious. It is your responsibility to communicate your message to the audience in the best possible way. To do this you need to know the readers' profiles and their needs.

We strongly suggest that you write down a list of who your reader groups are, and what you think they require from the report. This should be used as a guiding document throughout the writing process, and as such, it can help in answering any questions related to what to include and exclude in the report. It is not until you have determined your reader groups that you can decide about the form and contents of your report.

There may be several reader groups. Here is one way of categorising them.

- *Experts.* Experts are people with highly specialised theoretical and practical knowledge in one or several areas. Often they are professionals operating in research and development areas in the business world, or in academic environments.

- *Technicians.* Like experts, technicians have a high level of knowledge, but it is more often of a practical nature, and they normally operate and maintain the things that experts have designed and developed.
- *Executives and business professionals.* These make decisions on non-technical issues, e.g. business, legal, financial, or political issues. Typically they are non-specialists with little or no technical knowledge of the subject.
- *Non-specialists.* People with little or no technical knowledge of the subject.

Another possible reader is the prospective employer interested in hiring you. In addition to grades and interviews, an employer may study your project report since it demonstrates your written communication skills, and your abilities to undertake a larger project. Readers in this category will want to assure themselves that your presentation skills are up to their standard.

Once you have identified the reader group(s), you should analyse them to determine their level of background knowledge and experience in the subject, *and* their needs and expectations of the report. Although there might be other characteristics of importance, these two issues are essential to how the report is structured and the subject presented.

When analysing the knowledge of the readers, there is the potential problem of what to do when you realise that certain groups may lack certain knowledge in some area. If you do not provide that knowledge they might not be able to understand the report. On the other hand, if you do include it, other readers might find it too basic and frustrating to read. Much time will be spent on getting to the core of the topic. In general, you should keep the background as short as possible, so that less energy is spent on the part of least interest in the overall perspective. Your decisions should be related to the size of that reader group, and how important the information they need is in relation to the rest of the report. For each issue that you consider for inclusion in the background, ask yourself, is it a core issue, or is it peripheral? Again, it is important to stress early in your report what you are going to cover. The reader will then know what to expect. If you decide not to include the extra background, it is wise to point the non-specialised reader to good references where they can get the extra knowledge if necessary.

One of the basic requirements of a report is that there is enough detail for the reader to make sense of the knowledge produced in the project. It should also convince the reader, with logical reasoning, that the knowledge and results obtained are solid.

Let us give another example of needs and expectations. Think about the examiner and the supervisor, and their expectations and needs. They are both specialists with expertise in the topic, but they may have different concerns. For example, the examiner might be more concerned with the holistic view, methodology, readability and the overall quality of the report. Your supervisor, however, may be more concerned with the details of the project, and the details of the results. You should also think about the needs and expectations of other students, since they should also be able to read your report.

From the example we can see that reader groups have both different and common requirements. Satisfying conflicting requirements is a tricky issue that takes careful handling. Talk to your supervisor and/or examiner about this; they should be able to help. It is a difficult task to write all the sections of a report so that all reader groups can understand it. One way of approaching the problem is to write each section for the reader group(s) that has an interest in that section. By using headings and section introductions, you can inform the reader which part to read, which parts can be skipped, and where to go next in the report.

Once reader groups have been identified, you can start to tailor the presentation to the different groups. There are several ways of adapting the report. Here are some examples:

- *Add necessary information.* Make sure that key concepts are described in enough detail, and that there are no gaps in the reasoning. The reader should be able to follow the line of thought. Make sure that the information in the report is also at the right level of detail.
- *Omit unnecessary information.* While it is vital to include necessary information in the report, it is also important to omit information that does not serve any purpose. Unnecessary information only dilutes your message. Remember, maintain focus.
- *Add examples.* Including examples in the report is one of the best ways to help the reader understand complex scenarios, but the examples need to be adequate and at the right level, i.e. not too complex and not too simple. Too simple examples only confirm the obvious and are a waste of time and space. Non-specialists might not understand very technical examples. On the other hand, experts might not benefit from 'artificially constructed' examples that are not realistic, and which leave out important details.
- *Adjust your language.* This includes the style, structure and length of sentences, as well as the vocabulary. However, no matter what language style you choose, the goal is always the same: communication of your message in such a way that the reader can understand it without confusion.

14.3 Requirements of the Report

The report should be written so that it enables the reader to follow the chain of thought, to be able to make sense of the approach and apply the solution to a related problem elsewhere, and to verify your results and contribution. In this sense, it is not very different from conveying your message in any other form. A report should be:

- *Concise.* Delete unnecessary redundancy in your report – omit needless words, phrases and paragraphs.
- *Focused.* Only include things that are explicitly related to your project, and which are necessary in order to understand and evaluate your work.
- *Clear.* Avoid unnecessarily complicated terminology, and write at a level you are comfortable with.

- *Properly typeset.* If you are familiar with general rules and guidelines for typographical typesetting and formatting, you might consider individualising the typesetting of your report. If not, we strongly recommend that you use already developed templates.
- *Well structured.* Order the contents of your report in such a way that it reads well and the reader knows where to find things.
- *Well written.* The report should contain no spelling, grammatical or other language errors.

14.4   Structure of the Report

> *'Good order is the foundation of all things.'*
> *- Edmund Burke*

When it comes to structuring the report and defining an outline, you have to think about the order in which to present the different parts of your work. The reader should be able to understand your work with minimum of effort, and also form an opinion of your findings. The obvious question is what makes a structure a good one. Characteristically, a good report introduces the reader to the subject area, describes the problem clearly, and gives a detailed description of the methods and techniques used to solve the problem. Further, the report should include an analysis of the results, and the advantages and disadvantages of the techniques used for solving the problem.

There are several good ways to structure a report. The less experienced writer should probably avoid attempting to invent a completely new and unique way of structuring a report. A good exercise is to study a journal article in the subject area, either one suggested by your supervisor, or one that you consider well written. Not only will this model the structure of a report written by an experienced writer, but it may also demonstrate what is typical in the area.

In general, avoid writing chronological reports, i.e. do not adopt a story-telling style where your work is documented in the chronological order that results were achieved.

A basic outline of a report could look as shown in Fig. 14.1.

In long reports, or ones with a great deal of technical terminology, it may be useful to include an appendix named "Glossary of terms", but only if you think it will help the reader significantly.

In very long reports, it might also be worthwhile having an index of keywords included in the report.

14.4.1   Title Page

The title page should specify the title, author, date, degree awarded, department and university (and possibly, the supervisor and examiner). Note that your department may have a standard template for the title page.

```
Title page
Abstract
Acknowledgements
Table of contents
List of figures and tables (optional)

Part 1: Introduction and Background
Chapter 1: Introduction
Chapter 2: Background
Chapter 3: Problem description and problem statement

Part 2: Main body – Describing your work
Chapter 4: Theory (advanced preliminaries and/or
   theoretical part of solution).
Chapter 5: Description of approach and method(s) to solve the problem
Chapter 6: Result analysis

Part 3: Wrap-up
Chapter 7: Related work
Chapter 8: Conclusions
References (or Bibliography)
Appendices (optional)
```

Fig. 14.1 Example of a basic outline of a report

A good title should be short and descriptive, indicating the most distinct features of your work. A title that is inexact will not attract the target reader groups. To determine the descriptiveness of a proposed title, ask yourself the following questions:

- Does the title indicate the general subject area (e.g. database systems, AI)?
- Does the title indicate the problem within the subject area (e.g. resource allocation)?
- Does the title give an idea of your approach?

A title does not have to answer all these questions, but you should be able to answer "yes" to at least two of them. A common mistake is for titles to be too long. Be concise. If you need to, add a descriptive subtitle.

14.4.2 Abstract

An abstract is an overview or summary. For reports there are two types of abstract: descriptive and informative. A descriptive abstract presents the main topic, the purpose or goal, and the structure of the contents. A descriptive abstract does not contain a summary of facts or conclusions. In contrast, the informative abstract presents key facts, an overview of the problem, the context and your contribution.

It does not include a general background. In short, an informative abstract should include the key statements from the body of the report.

For thesis reports, the informative abstract should be one of the first pages, following the title page.

Most readers will decide from the abstract whether to spend precious time reading the rest of the report or not. Hence, it is important that the abstract is interesting, concise and informative. The abstract must be able to stand alone as an autonomous piece of text to allow the reader to understand it without searching through the rest of the report. For this reason you should avoid using references, acronyms, abbreviations or jargon specific to the subject area. However, an informative abstract is not an introduction to the topic, and it should not be seen as an introduction to the report. Do not, therefore, write introductory explanations of basic concepts (unless this is the focus of the thesis report).

Given this, we advocate that a good abstract should (1) give a high-level presentation of the subject area studied, (2) reason about the importance and why it is an interesting area worthy to be studied, (3) present a high-level description of the approach, and (4) summarise the contribution. An informative abstract should summarise all the major sections of the report, the key concepts, contributions, and conclusions. A typical abstract is about 250–500 words. This is not more than 10–20 sentences, so you will obviously have to choose your words very carefully in order to cover so much information in such a condensed format. You must therefore exclude any general and obvious statements; the phrasing should be concentrated and compact.

The abstract should be one of the last things, if not the very last thing, that you write. There is a good reason for this. It is not until you are close to finishing your project that you have a full picture of what has been achieved, and can write a precise and meaningful abstract. The abstract should be written in the same language as the rest of the report. However, if the report is written in a language other than English, you might consider including an abstract in English as well.

At the end of the abstract you could include a list of keywords to help the reader position the material with respect to the subject area and the problem under study. Keywords, in addition to the title, the list of authors and possibly the abstract, are normally included in library databases.

14.4.3 Chapter 1 – Introduction Chapter

A good report requires a good introduction which sets the scene by putting the work into a bigger perspective. This is normally best done by giving an overview showing how your subject area, e.g. databases, relates to the rest of the field of computer/information science. Within this context it is then easy to outline the key ideas of your work, in particular highlighting the benefits of your work. The introduction complements the abstract. It gives the information left out of the abstract. Normally, an introduction contains some or all of the following elements:

- *Topic* – indicating the specific topic of the report; this should be done as early as possible, preferably in the first paragraph of the report.
- *Purpose and situation* – indicating why the report was written and what the purpose was.
- *Target readers* – indicating for who the report is intended.
- *Topic background* – provides key definitions and basic preliminaries important to the reader; it should catch the reader's interest.
- *Overview of the report* – describes the general outline of the report. This informs the reader what to expect, and it makes it easier to understand your material, and to make the transitions between sections.

Check that these key elements are included when you revise the introduction chapter.

The introduction chapter should show which research community, if any, you want to be associated with, i.e. which community has done similar work before. You can do this by describing the most important related work in the area (with proper referencing).

The introduction can be seen as an extended abstract, and so it is generally a good idea to defer writing the introduction until the end of your project.

The introduction chapter prepares the reader for the whole report. However, in longer reports, individual chapters/sections might also need an introduction. These help the reader to understand the purpose of each section, and to position the contents in relation to the rest of the report. These section introductions share some common elements with the introduction chapter; they indicate the topic, give an overview of the contents, and provide a section orientation, all of which guide the reader.

14.4.4   Chapter 2 – Background

A reader who is familiar with the subject area should be able to skip this chapter without difficulties. Hence, this chapter should only present fundamental knowledge necessary in order to understand the problem (but not necessarily the solution). The problem will be described in detail in the successive chapters. Hence, it is best to avoid discussing specifics with respect to the problem, your solution and contribution in this chapter.

The hard thing about writing this section is to decide what the level of detail should be. This is where you can take advantage of the list of target readers you produced earlier. For each target group, list the subject areas you think the typical reader will need in order to appreciate your findings.

The purpose of these preliminaries is not to write a new textbook on the subject. If you feel that the chapter is getting too long, then the following actions are possible. Firstly, revise the list of subject areas to be covered, and only include the minimum set. Secondly, within the subject areas, give only the minimum material necessary to raise the reader to the desired level. Instead of including very basic material, you could refer the reader to good references (ones which are of high quality and easily accessible). A third approach might be to tailor the presentation to only the most important reader groups.

14.4.5 Chapter 3 – Problem Description and Statement

This chapter has two important objectives. It should (1) present the problem in a non-ambiguous way, both at a high level and in detail; and (2) show why the problem is important, justifying why it should be studied (after all, you do not want to study a problem that no one is interested in).

Describing the problem in detail entails declaring the aims and objectives (this was discussed in Chaps. 7 and 8 of this book), and outlining the existing constraints and assumptions that have been made regarding the problem.

14.4.6 Chapters 4–6 – The Core of your Report

These chapters describe and discuss (1) advanced preliminaries i.e. existing knowledge that the reader group may not be familiar with, but which is necessary in order to understand your solution (discussed in Chap. 7 of this book); (2) your approach and methods (discussed in Chaps. 7 and 8 of this book); and (3) your analysis of the results (discussed in Chap. 10 of this book). These chapters represent the core of your report.

Remember, a report should contain enough detail for the study to be repeated. The primary purpose of your report is to disseminate your findings or results. Your findings, then, should be described in enough detail for the reader to judge them. Further, there should be enough detail to make it possible to transfer any of your solutions elsewhere. For example, if you have developed a new algorithm for sorting numbers, others should be able to implement your algorithm in the future, either for sorting numbers in some application, or for using it as a baseline in a benchmark test of such algorithms.

14.4.7 Chapter 7 – Related Work

This chapter serves the purpose of positioning your work in the context of other people's work in the area. This chapter should include a comparison of your work with closely related efforts. It should demonstrate the principal differences and similarities with respect to (1) the details of the problem, (2) the approach, (3) the results, and possibly (4) the methodology. In particular, when you compare your approach with those of others, it is important that you objectively weigh the advantages and disadvantages. This increases your credibility and that of your study. Further, it will show that you did your homework, and that you know what the state-of-the-art in the area is. This will support and strengthen any claims of originality in your work.

It should be noted that there are both pros and cons to having a separate chapter covering related work close to the end of the report. On the positive side, it enables the author to do a very thorough and detailed comparison, with respect to the problem, the approach, and the results, without the risk of diluting the message. This is particularly useful if the number of approaches included in the comparison is large, since the discussions normally become be lengthy. Of course, the related work chapter should complement the other chapters. For example, if you want to report on the results of a new sorting algorithm, then you will have to compare its performance with some other sorting algorithms, and those should probably then be described in detail in the analysis chapter in order for the reader to appreciate your results.

When studying research reports, it is also common for related work to be included in the background chapter. This way, the expert reader can position the work within the subject area, by seeing which other efforts you consider relevant to your project. However, making a detailed comparison will be difficult since neither the problem, nor the approach or the results will have been described.

14.4.8 Chapter 8 – Conclusion

The conclusion chapter is the last section of the report, and it gives a summary of the report, presents conclusions and a final analysis, and possibly some afterwords, e.g. directions for future work. The conclusions section enables you to leave the reader with the right perspective on your work. This is particularly important as the length and the detail in the report increase.

First, a general rule for the conclusion chapter is that it should consist of reflections on the work. It should *not* present any new details of the approach or results etc., which have not been explained in previous chapters. This is not the time or place to surprise the reader (the report is not a novel where the least suspected person is found to be the murderer at the end).

The conclusion chapter should at least contain a brief overview of the purpose of the work and the problem studied. More importantly, it should have a summary that emphasises the main *contributions* and *results*, stressing why the results are valuable and putting them into the research context.

This is a good time to present your final conclusions. You present your interpretation of the results, or your recommended choice, e.g. of a model or a technique. This is particularly useful if you have compared different techniques or models, or if there are conflicting theories which may be difficult to interpret. Remember that you are now an expert on the topic, and the reader wants to know how you view the situation. All the conclusions presented in this last chapter should be backed up by the earlier parts of the report.

This is also a good place to elaborate on future developments, to outline interesting directions for future work and to discuss what remains to be done. You may also outline what you consider to be important to make the approach more generally applicable and/or how things can be improved. For example, you may discuss possible extensions to your solution, and identify relaxations of constraints and assumptions that were introduced to make the problem a bit easier to solve. You might also elaborate on solutions to other problems that were identified and discussed in the main body of the report.

It is often worthwhile making a distinction between future work that you might do, and future work that other people could look into (remember, you have studied the area for some considerable time, so your thoughts are of great interest). Note that a discussion on future work could potentially contain any number of suggestions, so keep focused, and discuss only the issues that in your mind are the most relevant and the most important. If the list is too long, then the reader might, unjustifiably, question whether you really did achieve something, or whether your list indicates that much of what was aimed for in the project still remains to be done.

It is also a well-known fact that there are two sections of a technical report that most readers will read before they actually decide to read the rest of the report. It should come as no surprise that most people read the abstract first, since its entire purpose is to give a high-level description of the work. However, the conclusion chapter is equally important in this sense, since it gives a more detailed explanation of the findings and contribution. Many readers, therefore, scan this chapter as well before they make the important decision as to whether to spend their precious time on reading your report or not. Remember this fact when you write the conclusion chapter (and the abstract as well, for that matter), and try to write it in such a way that an expert could read it independently of the rest of the report.

14.5   Style of the Report

It is generally a good idea to describe at the very beginning of a chapter what the purpose of the chapter is, and how you are going to present the material. In contrast to the case in fictional literature, you do not want to surprise the reader. Instead you want to prepare the reader for what is going to happen next, so that they can focus on understanding your project, as opposed to trying to figure out how the report is structured and what the objectives are, etc. So, make sure that you give an outline of the sections, since this represents your chain of thought.

In order to enhance understanding and readability of your report, it is of utmost importance that you are not vague or ambiguous in your descriptions. Make sure that sentences are not unnecessarily long, and that they are to the point. In scientific writing, it is generally considered good practice to avoid using personal pronouns, e.g. I, you, etc.

Be *precise* in your descriptions. This implies that hypotheses, arguments and results are formulated and separated in a non-ambiguous and distinct manner.

Furthermore, concepts and terminology should have one, and only one, distinct meaning that is used consistently throughout the report.

Be *concise* in your descriptions, i.e. ensure that arguments and hypotheses are expressed as efficiently as possible. Avoid words that do not add any meaning to your argument. In order to keep the report concise, make sure that all material is within the explicit focus of the project area.

Write for a *target reader group*, and make sure that this group will be able to understand the content easily. When making a choice between equally simple expressions, choose the most precise one. Similarly, when making a choice between equally precise expressions, choose the simplest one.

Be *structured/organised* in your presentation, i.e. make sure your report has a distinct outline.

14.6 Managing References

By properly referencing the material your work is based upon, you achieve several things: (1) you show how your work extends the current state-of-the-art knowledge in the area, (2) you show the originality of your work, (3) you give credit to other people's work (and avoid being accused of plagiarism), (4) you support and support arguments made in your report (any claim made in the report must be supported either by your own research or by citing the results published by other people), and (5) you show that you are familiar with the work done in the area.

Proper referencing includes how references are presented in the body of the text, and how references are presented in the reference list. This section covers the most common types of references/sources cited in research reports, and the information that needs to be included in the bibliographical entry in the reference list. Further, it shows different reference style systems and discusses how these are listed in the text, and how they should be presented in the reference list.

14.6.1 The List of References

The list is titled Bibliography or Selected Bibliography. If the list only includes references referred to in the text, then the list is titled Works Cited, Literature Cited, or References. Of these, the terms Bibliography and References are the most commonly used. Usually, only references that are referred to in the report are included.

The reference list contains bibliographical information about each source that has been cited in the report. Bibliographical information contains information about the reference such that it properly and uniquely identifies the source where the material was published. It should be precise enough to enable the reader to identify and locate the source.

Arranging the reference list as a single list ordered alphabetically is the most common, and also, usually, the best form. In Harvard style and Apalike style the list is ordered by the last name of the authors. This arrangement makes it simple to find references in the list. The rules for arranging the list are:

1. A single author entry comes before an entry having multiple authors starting with the same author.
2. Works by the same author are sorted chronologically, i.e. by publication date (alternatively they may be sorted alphabetically by title).

In some areas it is also common to list references in the same order as their first occurrence in the text. However, this is only appropriate when the reference is listed as a numerical in the citation in the body text.

Dividing the reference list into sections, e.g. based on the type of publication, where each section is sorted alphabetically, makes it more time consuming to find references in the list. The reader would have to know in which section to look, but this is not revealed by the citation.

14.6.2 Sources

There are several different types of sources that can be cited, each having their own set of bibliographical data. In this book we show how to properly manage the following types of references: journal articles, conference/workshop papers, books, doctoral theses, masters' dissertations, technical reports, web pages and interviews.

While this book uses the Harvard reference style, there are many other styles. In Sect. 14.6.3 we describe, in addition to the Harvard style, the APA style and the Vancouver style of referencing. For this purpose, we use the following set of example references:

Michael R. Blaha, William J. Premerlani, A. R. Bender, R. M. Salemme, M. M. Kornfein, and C. K. Harkins' conference article "Bill-of-Material Configuration Generation" appearing in the Proceedings of the Sixth International Conference on Data Engineering, 1990, pages 237–244.

Barry W. Boehm's book with the title "Software Engineering Economics", published 1981 by Prentice-Hall, Englewood Cliffs, New Jersey.

R. Davison and N. Kock's web resource *Professional Ethics*. Available from: http://www.is.cityu.edu.hk/research/resources/isworld/ethics/index.htm. The web resource was last updated in 2004 and it was accessed on 27 June 2007.

G. Khalifa, Z. Irani, L. P. Baldwin, and S. Jones' article "Evaluating Information Technology With You In Mind" appearing in The Electronic Journal of Information Systems Evaluation, volume 4, number 1. Available from: http://www.ejise.com/volume-4/volume4-issue1/issue1-art5.htm. It was accessed on 27 June 2007.

H. Kopetz and P. Verissimo's book chapter entitled "Design of Distributed Real-Time Systems", chapter 16 in the book "Distributed Systems" edited by S. Mullender. The book was published by Addison-Wesley in 1993.

Donald E. Knuth's well-known book "The Art of Programming" 3rd edition, vol 2, 1999 published by Addison-Wesley, Reading, MA, USA.

Stella Gatziu and Klaus R. Dittrich's book chapter entitled "SAMOS", chapter 12 (pages 233–247) in the book "Active Rules in Database Systems" edited by Norman W. Paton. The book was published by Springer-Verlag New York Inc. in 1999.

C. Douglass Locke's Ph.D. thesis entitled "Best-Effort Decision Making for Real-Time Scheduling". The thesis was submitted to the Department of Computer Science, Carnegie-Mellon University, May 1986. The thesis is available as a technical report with the number CMU-CS-86-134.

C. Douglass Locke's journal article "Software Architecture for Hard Real-Time Applications: Cyclic Executives vs. Fixed Priority Executives", Real-Time Systems Journal, vol 4:1, pages 37–53, 1992.

C. Mohan's conference article "Repeating History beyond ARIES" appearing in the Proceedings of the 25th International Conference on Very Large Data Bases, held in Edinburgh, Scotland, UK, September 7th–10th, 1999, pages 1–17. The conference proceedings were edited by M. P. Atkinson, M. E. Orlowska, P. Valduriez, S. B. Zdonik and Michael L.

Karl R. Popper's book "The Logic of Scientific Discovery" 2nd edition (reprint from 1959), published 1992 by London and New York, Routledge.

John A. Stankovic's article "Misconceptions About Real-Time Computing: A Serious Problem for Next-Generation Systems", appearing in the IEEE Computer, volume 21, number 10, October 1988.

John A. Stankovic's article "Real-Time Computing Systems: The Next Generation" appearing in the book "Hard Real-Time Systems". The book was published by IEEE Computer Society Press in 1988, and was edited by John A. Stankovic.

John A. Stankovic, Sang H. Son, and Jörgen Hansson's article "Misconceptions about Real-Time Databases" appearing in the IEEE Computer journal, pages 29–36, June 1999.

Note: The above is NOT a formatted reference list. It is only a listing of the references we use as examples in the following sub-chapters.

14.6.3   Reference Style

In this section we show the different ways to cite sources in the text, and how to build the reference list.

14.6.3.1   Harvard Style

In the body of the text:
Harvard style uses the form: author, date. In the text, the surname of the author and the year of the publication are given. The full biographical details are listed at the end of the report in the list of references.

Single author
There are two ways of referencing in the text. When the author's name naturally occurs in the sentence, the year is listed within parentheses just after the name. If the author's name does not occur naturally in the sentence, then both the name and the year are given within parentheses. For example,

> Knuth (1999) showed that....

or

> It has been shown that..... (Knuth, 1999).

Where a publication does not have an author, as in a corporate publication, for example, the author's name is replaced by the name of the corporation.

Multiple authors – two authors

When citing work with two authors, their surnames are listed. For example,

Gatziu and Dittrich's (1999) overview of the SAMOS project...

or

The SAMOS project investigated active object-oriented database features on top of a commercial database management system (Gatziu and Dittrich, 1999).

Multiple authors – more than two authors

When citing work with more than two authors, you should, in the body of the text, only list the first author and substitute the remaining author names with "et al.". This is an abbreviation for "et alia" meaning "and others" in this context. In the reference list you should include all author names (only when the author list is exceptionally long, for example 20 or more authors, should you consider using et al. in the reference list as well). For example,

Stankovic et al. (1999) identified common misconceptions about real-time databases.

or

Several misconceptions about real-time databases have been identified (Stankovic et al., 1999)...

Multiple references

When citing multiple references with the same author but with different publication years, you need only list the years, separated by ",". The order should be chronological. For example,

Locke (1986, 1992) showed that...

or

It has been shown that.... (Locke, 1986, 1992).

When citing multiple references with the same author and with the same publication year, you should add "a" for the first publication, "b" for the second one, etc. References are listed in order of importance. If all the references are equally important, they should be listed in chronological order. Further, when citing multiple references, by different authors, they are separated by ";". For example,

Real-time systems introduce additional technical issues due to the application time constraints that should be met (Stankovic, 1988a, 1988b; Stankovic, Son, and Hansson, 1999).

In the reference list, these references would appear as follows:

Stankovic, J. A. 1988a. Misconceptions About Real-Time Computing: A Serious Problem for Next-Generation Systems. *IEEE Computer*, 21(10), October, pp. 10–19.
Stankovic, J. A. 1988b. Real-Time Computing Systems: The Next Generation. In: Stankovic, J. A. (ed). *Hard Real-Time Systems*. IEEE Computer Society Press. 1988.
Stankovic, J. A., Son, S. H., and Hansson, J., 1999. Misconceptions About Real-Time Database Systems. *IEEE Computer*, 32(6), June, pp. 29–36.

References with page numbers in the body of the text
When making a reference to a particular statement in a book, it is often good practice to include additional information about where the statement can be found. For example, with direct quotations, include the page number where the quotation was found. This is particularly useful if the reference cited is a book or something similar. For example,

> Until quite recently the idea of simplicity has been used uncritically, as though it were quite obvious what simplicity is, and why it should be valuable (Popper, 1992, p. 136).

Bibliographical Data:
The reference list should be sorted in alphabetical order. Sorting references by type is not a good idea, since you would have to know the type of reference when scanning the reference list, and this is not given in the text. Ordering references according to their relative occurrence in the text is also a poor idea for similar reasons.

We now describe how the different types of references are written in the reference list. For each source we list the fields that should be included in the reference list, and give a few examples and comments. Try to use as many of these field as possible. However, in some cases you have to omit some fields since you lack information.

Book:
   Author(s)
   Year of publication
   Title – should be in *Italic*
   Edition – if it is not the first edition
   Publisher
   Place of publication
   Examples:

Boehm, B. W. 1981. *Software Engineering Economics*. Prentice-Hall, Eaglewood Cliffs, New Jersey.
Knuth, D. E. 1999. *The Art of Programming*. 3rd edition, vol 2, Addison-Wesley, Reading, MA, USA.
Popper, K. R. 1992. *The Logic of Scientific Discovery*. 2nd edition (reprint from 1959). Routledge, London and New York.

If the book has an editor instead of an author, you should cite the work the same way, except that in the reference list you should include the word "editor(s)", or its abbreviation "ed(s).", after the author name(s).

Chapter in an edited book:
In addition to the fields for a book, the following fields should also be included:

   Editor(s)
   Chapter
   Page numbers
   Examples:

Gatziu, S. and Dittrich, K. R. 1999. SAMOS. In: N. W. Paton, editor. Active Rules in Database Systems. Springer-Verlag, New York, chapter 12, pp. 233–247.

Kopetz, H. and Verissimo, P. 1993. Design of distributed real-time systems. In: S. Mullender, editor. *Distributed systems*, Addison-Wesley, chapter 16.

Journal article:
Author(s)
Year of publication
Title of the article
Name of journal – should be in *Italic*
Volume number, issue number, and/or month
Publisher
Page numbers of article

Examples:
Locke, C. D. 1992. Software Architecture for Hard Real-Time Applications: Cyclic Executives vs. Fixed Priority Executives. *Real-Time Systems Journal*, 4(1), pp. 37–53.
Stankovic, J. A. 1988a. Misconceptions About Real-Time Computing: A Serious Problem for Next-Generation Systems. *IEEE Computer*, 21(10), October, pp. 10–19.
Stankovic, J. A. Son, S. H., and Hansson, J., 1999. Misconceptions About Real-Time Database Systems. *IEEE Computer*, 32(6), June, pp. 29–36.

Conference paper:
Author(s)
Year of publication
Title of the paper
Editor(s) of the conference proceedings
Title of conference proceedings – should be in *Italic*
Location and dates of the conference
Publisher
Page numbers of paper

Examples:
Blaha, M. R., Premerlani, W. J., Bender, A. R., Salemme, R. M., Kornfein M. M., and Harkins, C. K. 1990. Bill-of-Material Configuration Generation. In *Proceedings of the Sixth International Conference on Data Engineering*, pp. 237–244.
Mohan, C. 1999. Repeating History beyond ARIES. In: M. P. Atkinson, M. E. Orlowska, P. Valduriez, S. B. Zdonik, M. L. Brodie, (eds) *Proceedings of the 25th International Conference on Very Large Data Bases*, Edinburgh, Scotland, UK, September 7th–10th, pp. 1–17.

Electronic documents (e.g. web pages)
The standard for citing electronic documents is yet to be set. The following shows a set of guidelines that are commonly used in practice when citing electronic documents, e.g. URL and CD-ROM documents. In general, the following should be included:

Author(s)
Year
Title – should be in *Italic*
Version number, if applicable
Type of medium – should be in square brackets, e.g. [online], [CD-ROM]
Publisher, if different from author

Place of publication, if applicable
Available from, e.g. URL
Access date (date when the document was viewed/downloaded)

Example:
Davison, R. and Kock, N., editors. 2004. *Professional Ethics* [online]. Available from: http://www.is.cityu.edu.hk/research/resources/isworld/ethics/index.htm[Accessed 27 June 2007].

For articles and papers from electronic journals published only on the Internet, the following should be included

Author(s)
Year
Title
Journal title – should be in *Italic*
Type of medium – should be in square brackets, i.e. [online]
Volume and/or issue number
Available from: URL address
Access date

Example:
Khalifa, G., Irani, Z., Baldwin, L. P. and Jones, S. 2001. Evaluating Information Technology With You In Mind. *The Electronic Journal of Information Systems Evaluation* [online], 4(1). Available from: http://www.ejise.com/volume-4/volume4-issue1/issue1-art5.htm [Accessed 27 June 2007].

It should be noted that to direct readers to an entire Web site (rather than a specific document on the site), it is sufficient to give the address of the site in a footnote. No reference entry is then needed. For example,

Sun's site[5] represents one of the most complete sites for describing Java in various aspects.

Dissertations and theses

Author
Year
Title
School
Department
Number (if applicable)

Example:
Locke, C. D. 1986. Best-Effort Decision Making for Real-Time Scheduling. Ph.D. thesis. Department of Computer Science, Carnegie-Mellon University. Technical report CMU-CS-86-134.

Interviews

For interviews that have not been published or broadcast, the following should be included:

---

[5] http://www.sun.com/

Name of interviewee
Name of interviewer
Description of type of interview
Place and date of interview

Example:
Smith, John. 2001. Interview by author. San Francisco, USA, 24 November.

Interviews that have been published should include the following additional information:
Type of medium – book, journal, radio program, television program, audio cassette, video cassette etc.
Editor, translator or director
Any additional information that is required to locate the source.

14.6.3.2   APA Style

One difference between APA style and Harvard, is that the abbreviation et al. is not used in the reference list, regardless of the number of authors. It can be used, however, in the parenthetical citation in the body of the text for material with three to five authors (after the initial citation, when all are listed) and in all parenthetical citations of material with six or more authors.

Basic form – single author

It has been shown that..... (Knuth, 1999).,
Knuth (1999) showed that....

or

In 1999, Knuth showed that...

Multiple authors
When citing work with two authors, then both authors are always listed. However, for references with more than two authors, then all the authors are listed when the first reference is made. For example,

Stankovic, Son, and Hansson (1999) identified common misconceptions about real-time databases.

or

Several misconceptions about real-time databases have been identified (Stankovic, Son, & Hansson, 1999)

All subsequent references use the abbreviated version where only the first author is listed while the remaining author names are replaced with the abbreviation et al. However, if a reference has more than six authors, the et al. format is used in the first occurrence as well (given that there is no ambiguity). The previous examples would now appear as follows:

Stankovic et al. (1999) identified common misconceptions about real-time databases.

or
> Common misconceptions about real-time databases have been identified (Stankovic et al., 1999)

When formatting references using the APA style, there are some things to remember. APA is more restrictive about capitalising words. The APA style recommends the following: you should capitalise only the first word of the title of the report and of any subtitle, if there is one. Further, you should capitalise names and significant words in the title of a journal (also true for book titles). The APA style also says that book titles and journal titles should be underlined.

Book

> Boehm, B. W. (1981). *Software engineering economics*. New Jersey: Prentice-Hall.
> Popper, K. R. (1992). *The logic of scientific discovery*. 2nd edition (reprint from 1959). London and New York, Routledge.

Books: include the edition statement (ex: 3rd ed. or Rev ed.) between the title and the place of publication if it is not the first edition. For example,
Knuth D. E. (1999). *The art of programming* (Vol. 2, 3rd ed.). Reading, MA: Addison-Wesley.

Chapter in an edited book

> Gatziu, S. & Dittrich, K. R. (1999). SAMOS. In: N. W. Paton (ed.), *Active Rules in Database Systems*. Chapter 12. Springer-Verlag, New York.
> Kopetz, H., & Verissimo, P. (1993). Design of distributed real-time systems. In: S. Mullender (ed.), *Distributed Systems*. Chapter 16. Addison-Wesley.

Journal article

> Locke, C. D. (1992). Software architecture for hard real-time applications: cyclic executives vs. fixed priority executives. *Real-Time Systems Journal*, 4(1), pp. 37–53.
> Stankovic, J. A., Son, S. H., & Hansson, J. (1999). Misconceptions about real-time database systems. *IEEE Computer*, 32(6), pages 29–36, June.

Conference paper

> Blaha, M. R., Premerlani, W. J., Bender, A. R., Salemme, R. M., Kornfein M. M., & Harkins, C. K. (1990). Bill-of-Material Configuration Generation. In: *Proceedings of the Sixth International Conference on Data Engineering*, pp. 237–244.
> Mohan, C. (1999). Repeating history beyond ARIES. In: *Proceedings 25th International Conference on Very Large Data Bases*, Edinburgh, UK, Sept. pp. 1–17.

Electronic documents (e.g. web pages)

> Davison, R. & Kock, N., editors. *Professional Ethics* [online], Available from: http://www.cityu.edu.hk/is/ethics/ethics.htm [Accessed 4 February 2002].

Articles and papers from electronic journals

> Khalifa, G., Irani, Z., Baldwin, L. P. & Jones, S. (2001). Evaluating Information Technology With You In Mind. *The Electronic Journal of Information Systems Evaluation* [online], 4(1). Available from: http://is.twi.tudelft.nl/ejise/vol4/papers/khalifia.htm [Accessed 4 February 2002].

Dissertations and theses

> Locke, C. D. (1986). Best-Effort Decision Making for Real-Time Scheduling. Doctoral thesis. Department of Computer Science, Carnegie-Mellon University. Available as technical report CMU-CS-86-134.

Interviews

Unpublished interviews do not need an entry in the reference list because they are what the APA calls "personal communications" and as such they do not provide recoverable data. Instead the interview is only listed within parentheses in the body of the text or in a footnote. For example,

(J. Smith, personal communication, November 24, 2001)

14.6.3.3 Vancouver Style

The Vancouver style, a.k.a. AMA style, was developed by the American Medical Association. As opposed to the author-date format used in Harvard, the Vancouver style uses a numerical format. Hence, in the text, the citation in the form of a number is included within square brackets. This makes referencing simple since there are no differences in citing a reference with one or multiple authors (c.f. Harvard and APA style). For example

It has been shown that..... [1].

or

Knut [1] showed that......

However, it is by some considered poor style to write as follows "In [1] it was shown…", so you should avoid this.

Similarly to the other styles discussed, the full biographical details are listed at the end of the report in the list of references. The bibliographical data for the sources are the same independently of the reference style used.

In the Vancouver style, author names are written using the initials of first and second names without spaces. They can include up to six authors. If there are more than six authors, include the first three, followed by et al. If no author is given, just start with the title.

Sources in the reference list are sorted in the order they are cited in the text. In a bibliography, hoever, entries are sorted by the last name of the author. When there are multiple references with the same author, these are sorted by the name of the second author, and by date if this is not applicable. In the example below we number the items consequtively, since we are not citing the references explicitly.

Book

[1] Boehm BW. *Software Engineering Economics*. New Jersey: Prentice-Hall; 1981.
[2] Popper KR. *The Logic of Scientific Discovery*. 2nd edition (reprint from 1959). London and New York, Routledge; 1992.

You should include the edition statement (e.g. 3rd ed. or Rev ed.) between the title and the place of publication, if it is not the first edition. For example,

[3] Knuth DE. *The Art of Programming*. Vol. 2, 3rd ed. Reading, MA: Addison-Wesley; 1999.

Chapter in an edited book

[4] Kopetz H, Verissimo P. Design of Distributed Real-Time Systems. In: Mullender S, ed. *Distributed Systems*. Addison-Wesley; 1993:chapter 16.

Journal article
Journal titles should be abbreviated if possible (given that there is a consensus on their abbreviation). Further, if the journal does not paginate continuously through the volume, include the month (and day, of available).

[5] Locke, CD. Software Architecture for Hard Real-Time Applications: Cyclic Executives vs. Fixed Priority Executives. *Real-Time Systems Journal*, 1992; 4(1): 37–53.

Conference paper

[6] Mohan, C. Repeating History beyond ARIES. In: Proc. 25th International Conference on Very Large Data Bases, Edinburgh, UK, Sept. 1999. p. 1–17.

Electronic documents (e.g. web pages)

[7] Davison, R., Kock, N., eds. Professional Ethics. [online], 2004. Available from: http://www.is.cityu.edu.hk/research/resources/isworld/ethics/index.htm. Accessed 27 June 2007.

Articles and papers from electronic journals

[8] Khalifa, G., Irani, Z., Baldwin, L. P., Jones, S. Evaluating Information Technology With You In Mind. *The Electronic Journal of Information Systems Evaluation* [online], 2001; 4(1). Available from: http://www.ejise.com/volume-4/volume4-issue1/issue1-art5.htm. Accessed 27 June 2007.

Dissertations and theses

[9] Locke CD. Best-Effort Decision Making for Real-Time Scheduling. Doctoral thesis. Department of Computer Science, Carnegie-Mellon University, May 1986. Available as technical report CMU-CS-86-134.

14.6.3.4 Other Recommendations

You should always try to read the original source, and avoid referencing a secondary reference. A secondary source represents another author's interpretation. It is possible that you would interpret the original source differently. Given that this could be a source of misunderstanding and error, you should avoid this as much as possible.

There are, however, occasions when it is not possible to study the original source, e.g. when the original source is no longer available, or the original source is written in a language you do not understand. In this case you must trust a secondary source, but you must indicate to the reader that this is a secondary source by citing it. It goes without saying that listing a reference that you have not studied yourself is the same as cheating.

Sometimes you may find that the number of references is too large, or that the same reference is listed frequently in a section. In this case, consider mentioning your source at the beginning of the section, and stress that your study is based on that source unless explicitly stated otherwise. This requires you to make it very clear in the text which observations and reflections are yours, and which are those of others.

14.6.4   References to Tables and Figures

Another type of reference in a report points to tables and figures. When referring to tables and figures in your text, avoid phrases such as "The data are shown in the table below". The problem with this type of reference is that it is dependent on the position of the table. It is called a *relative* reference, since the word "below" in the reference is dependent on the position of the table relative to the reference. When making the final corrections to your report, you are very likely to move some tables and figures to make the report look nicer. It is very easy in this situation, to forget to update relative references, and very time-consuming to look for them in the text.

A better way of referencing figures and tables is by *absolute* references, which are independent of position. An example might be: "The data of the simulations are shown in Table 10.1". Since the table number (10.1) is used, it does not matter if the table appears before or after the phrase containing the reference. It may also appear on another page, since it is still easy to locate it with the help of the table numbers. However, it is best to keep the table or figure as close as possible to the place in the text where the reference appears. It is tiring for the reader to have to flip back and forth through the pages to alternately read the text and look at the table or figure. In general, it is somewhat better to have tables and figures after the first occurrence of a reference to them, rather than before.

15
Examination

15.1 The Examiner's Roles

The role of the examiner is to examine and evaluate the performance of the student and the results of the project. In Sect. 3.3 we outlined two typical roles that an examiner can take, i.e. quality evaluator and quality assuror. Depending on which role the examiner takes, it will affect his or her options for setting a grade for a student project.

When acting as a quality evaluator, the examiner usually listens to a final presentation by the student and reads the final report. This has the advantage that the examiner only sees the final "product" and can evaluate the student only on the final achievements. This is fair, in the sense that it is the final product that matters, and any problems the student may have had along the way will not influence the grade if the final product is a good one.

When acting as a quality assuror, the examiner will meet the student (and the supervisor) at different stages of the process. This has the advantage that the examiner gets more insight into the process. For example, if the examiner is present at initial presentations, where the students present the aims and objectives of their projects, this can give valuable information for evaluating the outcome of the projct. Projects that fail, or face severe difficulties, often do so because the aims and objectives were formulated vaguely or not chosen carefully. The student may later "repair" this in the final report, by updating the description of aims and objectives, but meet with difficulty because of the problems with the initial aims and objectives. On the other hand, the examiner may find it difficult to view the work afresh, uninfluenced by his or her previous judgement of earlier versions of the report or the work.

When acting as a quality assuror, the examiner may find that he or she is taking on a supportive role, rather than an evaluative role. This can be difficult for a number of reasons. Any advice given by the examiner may later come back to him or her. For example, if the examiner advises a student to include item X in the list of objectives, the examiner will later have the role of evaluating the "wisdom" of including item X among the objectives. It then becomes difficult for the examiner to criticise the student for including this item. On the other hand, the examiner will may also not want to give the student credit for including item X, since it was the

145

M. Berndtsson et al. (eds.), *Thesis Projects: A Guide for Students in Computer Science and Information Systems.*
© Springer 2008

examiner's own suggestion to include it. The "solution" to this dilemma may even be to reduce the students' grade on the grounds of "lack of independence". In conclusion, the result of the examiner's well-meaning advice to the student is a reduced grade!

There is no obvious solution to this dilemma, and our suggestion is merely to be aware of it. When giving advice on a project, the examiner may want to make this dilemma clear to the student and explain clearly what the consequences are. The advice can still be useful, as a way of "reviving" a project. The result may be a rescued or more successful project, even though the inclusion of a particular item as a consequence of the examiner's advice may not be rewarded.

Another possible solution is to give advice in a more general and indirect way. For example, rather than giving concrete advice to "include item X among your objectives", a more general discussion can be held with the student to encourage his or her thought processes to become more creative. The result may be that the student discovers the idea of including item X himself or herself, or some other idea which is equally (or more) fruitful.

15.2   What to Examine

The assessment criteria to be used in deciding the grade for the project should be clear both to the examiner and to the student. The examiner should have a set of explicit criteria, since this reduces the amount of subjectivity. It is also the easiest way of motivating and explaining a grade to a student. The student should know beforehand what criteria are to be applied, since it gives a set of goals or standards of quality to strive for.

The syllabus for a project course is likely to have a list of expected "learning outcomes" or "expected knowledge outcomes". In such cases, these should correspond well with the criteria used by the examiner when setting a grade. If the course aims to develop a certain set of skills, then student grades should reflect to what degree the student has acquired those skills.

When the examiner develops the set of criteria, some pitfalls must be avoided. Firstly, different criteria should not overlap too much. Secondly, there should be no large gaps in what is covered, i.e. the set of criteria taken together should cover all aspects of what is important as skills resulting from the course. Thirdly, any weighting scheme used for calculating grades should be chosen very carefully. In fact, it may not be necessary to use a particular formula for calculating grades, but rather to use the criteria only as a structure for thinking about the grade and for developing one's motivations for a chosen grade.

It is also important to pay attention to the fact that a form of weighting can be introduced implicitly by choosing, for example, more criteria that evaluate the report than those that evaluate the defence. The example in Fig. 15.1 includes six criteria regarding the report, and only two regarding the defence, thus implicitly giving more weight to the report – especially if the grade is decided by a simple summation scheme.

In Fig. 15.1 an example set of assessment criteria is given. These should not be copied without carefully checking to what degree they correspond to the course at hand, checking what must be deleted and what must be added. Ideas for further criteria can be found in other sources, for instance in the refereeing criteria for conferences and journals.

One suggested way of using such criteria is to print them on forms, leaving some space in between. This allows, for each student and for each criterion, a grade to be written (for example, Fail, Pass, or Excellent), together with a short justification for the grade. Justifications can include examples of mistakes, or of demonstrated skill. The completed form can be used by the examiner to decide an overall grade, to discuss or justify the grade with the supervisor, and finally to present the grade to the student.

General

- Relevance of chosen topic
- Originality of chosen topic
- Significance of findings
- Degree to which the work is the student's own work (as opposed to the supervisor's)

Report

- Clarity of presentation
- Consistency between different parts of the report
- Degree of insight apparent from the arguments presented to support the choices that the student has made
- Ability to differentiate between others' thoughts and own
- Ability to handle references and citations
- General stylistic impression

Defence

- Degree of insight apparent from the arguments presented to support claims and conclusions
- Degree of insight apparent from discussion in response to relevant questions

Others

- How the students performed as opponent
- Fulfilment of deadlines and other formal requirements

Fig. 15.1 Example set of assessment criteria

The final point in the preceding paragraph is not the least important one: a student who sees evidence that the examiner has made a thorough evaluation and has good arguments is more likely to accept the grade awarded. Also, if any discussion or complaint arises, having the examiner's judgement in writing in a structured form can be a good way of avoiding misunderstandings.

Given the defined criteria for evaluation, the main work of the examiner is of course to read and evaluate the report. Together with the criteria, it can be of help to use the questions from sub-section 12.2.2 during detailed reading of the report, as a guide to what to look for in the report. However, the examiner's role is different from that of the opponent. There are factors which do not serve as a basis for relevant opponent questions, but which are important for the examiner to consider when evaluating the work. Examples can be found in the "Report" section of the criteria listed in "Ability to handle references and citations". As an opponent, it is not very relevant to ask "Why did you not list the page numbers of any articles in your reference list?" but such mistakes should certainly be included in the examiner's evaluation of the work.

When the role of opponent is taken by fellow students, it is normally because acting as opponent is a part of the course. This may also entail that the student's performance as opponent should be taken into account by the examiner when deciding the student's grade for the course. If so, the examiner must probably attend the presentation where the student is acting as opponent – regardless of whether the presenting student has a different examiner. It also means that the examiner must take note of the opponent's performance during the defence. This can be particularly difficult if one is (at the same time) making notes on the performance of the defending student, and at the same time asking questions of the defending student.

One way of making the examiner's task a little easier is to ask opponents to hand in a sheet before the presentation with the questions they plan to use. In this way, one can concentrate on taking notes of the performance of the defending student during the defence. It also means that one has more insight into how carefully each opponent has read the report of the defending student, and how well each opponent prepared beforehand.

There are a number of reasons for evaluating a student's performance as opponent and including this in the student's grade for the course. It serves, for instance, as a test of whether the student has sufficient understanding of the subject area in which he or she is taking a degree. To prepare a good opposition with relevant questions requires a good understanding of the subject in general. This is perhaps especially so for the opposition of a successful project. In a badly written report, it is easy to find good questions relating to the weaknesses of the report, but in a very well written report on work which has been well executed, the task of finding the right questions to ask is of a different level of difficulty, and requires perhaps a deeper understanding. Put another way, the more advanced the work, the more advanced the questions needed; this of course requires more knowledge.

Another reason to evaluate the student's performance as opponent is that it serves as a strong incentive to perform the task well, and should thus make the student read the report more carefully. Careful and critical reading of another student's work can make a student understand his or her own work, i.e. its strengths and weaknesses, better than before. Comments the student may have received about a certain weakness in his or her own work may be better understood if he or she sees the same mistake being made by another student – especially when having the task of criticising it!

Some thought may be given to how presenters and opponents are paired. The examiner may want to make sure, for instance, that a student who undertook a project about real-time systems has the ability to explain the work to someone who is generally knowledgeable in computer science, but who knows nothing about real-time systems. This can be a good test to see whether the student knows the fundamental concepts in real-time systems well enough to explain them to those who are not in the same field. Similarly, the examiner may want to pair students who have performed very well with ones who have performed badly. Work with many weaknesses may benefit from helpful comments from one of the most skilled and knowledgeable students.

In the evaluation of opponent performance, it is important to keep in mind the opponent's role. In other words, the evaluation criteria must correspond with the guidelines given for opposition.

Here follows a list of questions which can be useful for an examiner while reading a report, and which can be used in addition to those already listed in sub-section 12.2.2.

Title, abstract, and introduction.

- Does the title of the report correspond well to its contents?
- Does the abstract give a complete and correct picture of the contents of the report?
- Can the abstract be understood without having to read all parts of the report beforehand?
- Does the introduction explain clearly and immediately what the investigated problem is?
- Does the introduction give a complete picture of the project, so that it could be read as a "mini-report" giving a brief overview of the whole project?

Problem statement.

- Does the author explain all terminology in a clear and precise way?
- Are terms used in a consistent way, or do some definitions seem to change over time?
- Does the author make use of relevant scientific conventions in the choice of terminology and definitions?

Methods.

- Is the description of the method sufficiently clear and detailed to allow replication?
- Are there any technical flaws, where a given method is applied in an incorrect way?

Results and analysis.

- Is the presentation of results focused on the relevant results, or does the author use a lot of space in the report on presenting data that are irrelevant to the defined problem?
- Are all analysis techniques used by the author applied in a correct way?
- Has the author chosen relevant analysis techniques, given the type of data and the defined problem?
- Are tables and figures used in a correct and relevant way?
- Does the author present all results in an objective way, or is there a subjective selection of only those results which support the author's claims?
- Do all text sections discussing results correspond to the actual results, i.e. is the author objective in the description of the results presented?

Conclusions.

- Does the author draw reasonable conclusions, or is there a tendency to exaggerate the importance of the findings?
- Are the arguments scientifically valid, or do they contain too much speculation?
- Is the summary of results well written, or is it simply a repetition with the same phrases as were used in the results and analysis sections?

References.

- Is the list of references syntactically correct?
- Are there any sources which are cited in the text, but which do not appear in the list of references?
- Are all citations in the text done in a syntactically correct way?
- Does the author use a good style in placing citations and referring to them in the text?
- Has the relevant literature been covered, or does there seem to be important gaps in the literature used?

Bibliography

Anon, 1993. *The Chicago Manual of Style.* 14th edition, Chicago, University of Chicago Press.

Denzin, N.K. and Lincoln, Y.S., editors, 1994. *Handbook of Qualitative Research.* Sage, Thousand Oaks.

Ebert, J., Suttenbach, R., and Uhe, I., 1997. Meta-CASE in practice: a case for KOGGE. In: A. Olivé and J. A. Pastor, editors. *Advanced Information Systems Engineering: 9th International Conference, CAiSE'97.* Barcelona, Catalonia, Spain, June 16–20 1997, Springer, Berlin, pp. 203–216.

Foster, A. 2004. A nonlinear model of information-seeking behavior. *Journal of the American Society for Information Science and Technology.* 55(3), 228–237.

IFIP WG 8.2. *Scope and Aims of IFIP WG 8.2, at* http://www.ifipwg82.org/scope.html (December 15, 1996).

Jain, R., 1991. *The Art of Computer Systems Performance Analysis: Techniques for Experimental Design, Measurement, Simulation, and Modeling.* John Wiley & Sons, New York, NY, USA.

Kuhlthau, C. 1993. *Seeking Meaning: A Process Approach to Library and Information Services.* Norwood, Ablex, cop.

Lee, A. S., 2001. Challenges to qualitative researchers in information systems. In: E. M. Trauth, editor. *Qualitative Research in IS: Issues and Trends.* IDEA group publishing, Hershey, PA, USA, pp. 240–270.

Limberg, L. 2000. Is there a relation between information seeking and learning outcomes? In: C. Bruce and P. Candy, editors. *Information Literacy : Advances in Programs and Research.* Wagga Wagga, Charles Sturt University Centre for Information Studies, pp. 193–207.

Maansaari, J. and Iivari, J., 1999. The evolution of CASE usage in Finland between 1993 and 1996. *Information & Management.* 36(1):37–53.

Marton, F. 2000. The practice of learning. *Nordisk pedagogik.* 20(4):230–236.

Orlikowski, W. J., 1993. CASE tools as organizational change: investigation incremental and radical changes in systems development. *Management Information Systems Quarterly.* 17(3):309–340.

Post, G. and Kagan, A., 2000. OO-CASE tools: an evaluation of Rose. *Information and Software Technology.* 42(6):383–388.

Sampaio, P. R. F., and Paton, N. W., 1997. Deductive object-oriented database systems: a survey. In: A. Geppert and M. Berndtsson, editors, *Proceedings of the 3rd International Workshop on Rules in Database Systems,* Vol 1312 in Lecture Notes in Computer Science, Springer, pp. 1–19.

Talja, S. 2002. Information sharing in academic communities: types and levels of collaboration in information seeking and use. *New Review of Information Behavior Research.* 3:143–160.

Tichy, W. F., 1998. Should computer scientists experiment more? 16 excuses to avoid experimentation. *IEEE Computer.* 31(5):32–40.

Walsham, G., and Waema, T., 1994. Information systems strategy and implementation: a case study of a building society. *ACM Transactions on Information Systems.* 12(2):150–173.

Wilson, T. 1999. Exploring models of information behaviour: the uncertainty project. *Information Processing and Management.* 35:839–849.

Wilson, T. 2000. Human information behaviour. *Informing Science.* 3(2):49–56.

Yin, R. K., 1994. *Case Study Research, Design and Methods.* 2nd edition, Newbury Park, Sage Publications.

Appendix

Some things you just should not do!

Some ways of making sure the supervisor regrets taking you on as a student:

- You avoid having meetings with your supervisor and keeping the supervisor up to date on the current status of your project, particularly in those phases of your project where communication is crucial to its outcome. Further, you do not inform your supervisor that the project is getting behind schedule.
- You give only brief responses, e.g. "it is under control", "just fine" to your supervisor when asked how the project is coming along. In the worst case, after a long period of time you go to your supervisor and say "nothing is working any more... I don't know what to do..."
- You miss scheduled meetings without previously informing your supervisor.
- You consult friends and other students, asking for their advice on important matters, rather than consulting your supervisor.
- You have an excessive use of different terms with the same meaning in your discussions, report, and presentation just to have variation.
- You develop a solution/implementation etc. first, then define a problem that fits what you have developed.
- When writing the literature analysis, you enthusiastically document the process and any adventures experienced when searching for related literature in the library.
- You ask your supervisor, at short notice, for detailed comments on a lengthy report, and require feedback within a day or two.
- You hand in reports that have severe presentation problems, e.g. bad grammar and spelling, due to the fact that your reports have not been proofread.
- You hand in revised versions of your report without marking changes made in the document since its previous version.
- You present failed projects as being a consequence of failure on your supervisor's part (while successful projects are, of course, always due to your own brilliant effort as a student).

Some ways of making sure the students regret having you as a supervisor:

- You only give the student short and general comments like "looks good", avoiding being specific about what you found particularly good.
- You only give the student general comments like "does not look good" without specifying what the student did wrong and what is expected.
- You give vague, imprecise and inconsistent comments to the student.
- You repeatedly change your opinion back and forth between meetings.
- You constantly show up late and unprepared for scheduled meetings.
- You miss scheduled meetings without previously informing the student.
- You present failed projects as being a consequence of a failure on the student's part (while successful projects are, of course, always due to your own brilliant efforts as a supervisor).

Some ways of making sure the supervisor and/or student will be upset with you as an examiner:

- You regularly give judgements of a very positive nature at the checkpoints, and at the final evaluation point out big weaknesses in the work and inform the student and the supervisor that you will not be recommending a pass grade for the student.
- You set a grade but are not able to justify it.

Bibliographies available on the Internet

In this section we focus on good information sources freely available on the Internet, since everyone with an Internet connection can reach them. Many other useful bibliographies are available. All URLs were collected in June 2007, and may change with time.

ACM Digital Library. ACM stands for Association for Computing Machinery. It maintains a large digital library containing papers on all aspects of computer science, which is searchable after registration (at no cost). The database contains bibliographic information, abstracts and reviews for articles published in ACM periodicals and proceedings since 1985. If you are a member of the ACM, you will also have access to articles in full-text (mostly in PDF).

URL: http://portal.acm.org/dl.cfm

Cogprints. Cognitive Sciences Eprint Archive. Contains papers in areas such as *"psychology, neuroscience, and linguistics, and many areas of computer science (e.g. artificial intelligence, robotics, vision, learning, speech, neural networks), philosophy (e.g. mind, language, knowledge, science, logic), biology (e.g. ethology, behavioral ecology, sociobiology, behaviour genetics, evolutionary theory), medicine (e.g. psychiatry, neurology, human genetics, imaging), anthropology (e.g. primatology, cognitive ethnology, archeology, paleontology), as well as any other por-*

tions of the physical, social and mathematical sciences that are pertinent to the study of cognition".

URL: http://cogprints.soton.ac.uk/

The Collection of Computer Science Bibliographies. This database contains several different computer science bibliographies, together with more than one million references. They are easily searchable by author, title, subject, conference etc.

URL: http://liinwww.ira.uka.de/bibliography/

Computer Science Technical Reports. The focus of this bibliography is on technical reports from around the world, containing more than 45,000 technical reports, often also Ph.D. theses.

URL: http://www.nzdl.org/

DBLP Bibliography. This database contains bibliographic information on more than 870,000 articles. Most of the articles are related to database systems, logic programming and associated areas.

URL: http://dblp.uni-trier.de/

HCI Bibliography. Human-computer interaction resources. It lists conference papers, books, reports, journal articles and also conference information, journal information and Internet links. Contains over 37,000 records in the human-computer interaction area. The search strategy is a bit tricky, but once you get the hang of it, it is quite good.

URL: http://www.hcibib.org/

IEEE Computer Society Digital Library. Another bibliography issued by a big organisation, containing references to articles from journals, magazines and conferences published by IEEE. The abbreviation stands for Institute of Electrical & Electronics Engineers.
Searching the bibliography is free, but you will have to pay for full-text access (in HTML).

URL: http://www.computer.org/portal/site/csdl/

SpringerLink. Bibliographic database from Springer-Verlag, including literature from volumes published in the series Lecture Notes in Computer Science. Many different aspects of computer science are covered, with several conference proceedings included in the series.

URL: http://www.springerlink.com/computer-science/

ResearchIndex. This bibliography indexes over 150,000 computer science articles from books, journals, conference proceedings and technical reports. The main benefit with this bibliography is the ability to get access to some of the articles in full-text, and also the possibility of viewing all citations made in a specific paper.

URL: http://citeseer.ist.psu.edu/

Uncover. This bibliography gives you access to almost 9 million references from over 18,000 journals and magazines in different areas, not only computer science. May be helpful anyway, but count on some information overload.

URL: http://www.ingenta.com/

Index

Printed in the United Kingdom
by Lightning Source UK Ltd.
129801UK00003B/142-144/A